Railway Memo

C000302455

BRADFORD

ALAN WHITAKER & BRIAN MYLAND

With photographs by Tom Allatt, Robert Anderson, G.H.Butland, Douglas Butterfield, Stephen Chapman, J.C.W.Halliday, J.C.Hillmer, John Holroyd, D.Ibbotson, M.A.King, Michael Leahy, Barry Mounsey, Peter Rose, John Rothera, Keith Preston, Malcolm Roughley, Peter Sunderland, Alan Thompson, Roy Wood.

BELLCODE BOOKS
10 RIDGE BANK TODMORDEN
LANCASHIRE OL14 7BA

Published by Bellcode Books.

Edited by Stephen Chapman.

Associate editor: Peter Rose.

Printed by the Amadeus Press Ltd., Huddersfield.

Typeset by Ryburn Book Prodn, Keele University, Newcastle-under-Lyme.

The ex-LMS 2-6-4Ts were synonymous with Bradford, being prolific performers on main line trains from both Exchange and Forster Square stations right up to the end of steam. Here, Fairburn tank No.42142 storms the bank through St Dunstan's with the 09.00 to Kings Cross via Leeds Central on 31st May, 1966. *(Brian Myland)*

FRONT COVER: The south exit from Bradford as it used to be before the Interchange was thought of. The ugly cladding hides the true appeal of the old Exchange station's magnificent arched roof on 17th August, 1961 as Low Moor Black Five No.44695 departs with an express for beyond the Pennines. On the extreme right is Vicar Lane goods warehouse. *(Peter Rose)*

FRONTISPIECE: Back in the 1930s Bradford handled vast amounts of freight. On the LNER section, J50 0-6-0T No.1041 (8960 from 1946) negotiates the south curve of the St Dunstan's triangle and heads for the Queensbury line with a transfer freight from Laisterdyke on 5th May, 1937. *(G.H.Butland)*

BACK COVER (TOP): Crewe-based Black Five No.45034 is steam tight, has a tender of decent coal and is set for a good run from Forster Square with the 5.10pm to Morecambe on 13th July,1961. The huge Valley Road wool warehouse looms above. *(Roy Wood)*

BACK COVER (BOTTOM): Low Moor was always an attraction to enthusiasts and no wonder, given the variety of motive power to be found there. On 18th July, 1961 ex-LNER Class 04/8 2-8-0 No.63864 was keeping company with L&Y 3F 0-6-0 No.52515. *(Peter Rose)*

INTRODUCTION

Looking at Bradford today it is hard to see that this great Yorkshire city was once a bustling railway centre driven by wool, commerce and engineering.

There are now just three routes into its two stations. They have been stripped of virtually all sidings and depots while acres of railway land have been redeveloped beyond recognition. Only local passenger trains now serve Bradford along with a rudimentary InterCity link to London, a couple of daily parcels trains and no freight.

Yet, little over 30 years ago the wool capital of the world sent main line expresses to three London termini as freight trains tripped busily between its five main goods depots, each one of which had its own huge warehouse devoted to the storage and distribution of wool. They served iron works, coal depots and scrapyards too, while local passenger trains linked a network of suburban stations.

Shipley and Low Moor provided a wealth of interest with all manner of trains passing through, while the Queensbury lines over the hills to Halifax and Keighley held a fascination of their own.

To the end of steam, Bradford maintained an interesting mix of motive power resulting from the time when the Midland, Great Northern and Lancashire and Yorkshire Railways vied for its custom.

In 1967 its steam-hauled portions of London expresses and neck and neck depar-

CONTENTS

tures of summer Saturday trains to the coast were a magnet for railway photographers.

In **Railway Memories No.4** over 200 of their superb photographs recall the time when the Bradford area (which we have stretched to Armley Moor in Leeds to meet up with Railway Memories No.3) was alive with railways and steam. It is not a history book, others fulfill that role, but a journey back to the days before the magnificent Exchange station gave way to the Interchange, the days when the Devonian left Forster Square for the sunnier end of the country, and the days when freight was the backbone of Bradford's railway business.

The Devonian to Paignton was one of the principal expresses from Forster Square. The last steam-hauled Devonian ran on 29th April, 1967 when Black Five No.44824 was photographed making a dramatic start on the short run to Leeds City where it would hand over to diesel power. *(Michael Leahy)*

SETTING THE SCENE

It took almost 50 years to develop Bradford's railway network but barely 15 to tear out its heart, and what remains today represents only a fragment of what was once a complicated system of lines radiating from the city.

Bradford's situation in a bowl-shaped depression surrounded by hills set the Victorian railway builders a tough challenge and resulted in the area boasting some of the most spectacular railway engineering in the West Riding.

Apart from the flat northern gateway into Airedale, all other lines were characterized by steep gradients which in steam days required sterling efforts by locomotives and crews to keep trains on the move.

In spite of its growing importance as an industrial and trading centre, it took Bradford until the 1840s to secure a place on the railway map.

Several attempts by the business community to give the city a railway in the 1830s all foundered due to lack of support, nor could the North Midland Railway be persuaded to extend its new Derby–Leeds line there. Its engineer, George Stephenson, advised the Bradfordians to form their own company but again they failed to win enough support and their great rival, Leeds, was first with a through link to London.

Spurred on by the high cost of transporting wool by road, Bradford's businessmen kept trying and in 1843 succeeded in forming their own company, with Railway King George Hudson as chairman.

In July the following year, they obtained Parliamentary powers for the Leeds and Bradford Railway between Leeds Wellington Street and Bradford via Shipley. With it was a short line to Leeds Hunslet Lane, providing direct connections to the south.

The Midland Railway, the North Midland's successor, also turned down the chance to extend its line so Stephenson was appointed engineer for the Leeds and Bradford and work began almost immediately.

The public opening was on 1st July, 1846 with the Bradford terminus being just east of Forster Square. Hourly services were introduced to Leeds and through trains started running to London Euston via Derby and Rugby.

This breakthrough sparked a flurry of railway building in the area which continued until the mid-1880s, providing Bradford with key routes to East Lancashire, Manchester and Merseyside via the Lancashire and Yorkshire Railway, London St Pancras, the North and Scotland via the Midland, which did eventually take over the Leeds and Bradford, and London Kings Cross via the Great Northern Railway.

Of the early lines into the city, the L&Y's route from Halifax via Low Moor, opened in 1850, was especially daunting, requiring major tunnels at Bowling, Wyke and Beacon Hill, plus a viaduct at Lightcliffe.

Other lines under construction in the 1850s included the GNR Leeds–Bradford route, opened in 1854, one from Laisterdyke to Ardsley via Morley, completed in 1857 and linking up with the Wakefield–Leeds West Yorkshire Railway (absorbed by the GNR in 1865), and the direct Laisterdyke–Bowling Junction route, also opened 1854 and enabling Leeds–Halifax trains to avoid a time–consuming reversal at Bradford.

By this time the city had three main stations. The original Midland terminus was replaced in 1890 by the much bigger Market Street which was renamed Forster Square in 1924. It had six platforms spanned by an overall roof and its own hotel. Apart from the owning company, the North Eastern Railway had a booking office there for selling tickets to Harrogate and, in the summer, to Scarborough via Leeds. Services such as these brought NER engines to Forster Square.

The station was demolished in 1992 after being replaced two years earlier by a new three-platform railhead which was intended to form an integral part of a £90 million shopping centre. The centre was to have been built on the site of the old station and goods yard but foundered in the 1990 property slump.

The GNR opened Adolphus Street on 1st August, 1854 but soon realised that it was too far out of the city centre, passengers preferring to use the more convenient Midland station.

As a result, the GNR agreed to share the L&Y's Drake Street station which was enlarged as part of the deal. The GNR also had to build a new line down to the L&Y at Mill Lane.

Bradford's first railway was the line from Leeds via Shipley, opened in 1846 by the Leeds and Bradford Railway which soon became part the Midland Railway. It terminated at a site east of Forster Square station which was not itself opened, to cope with increasing traffic levels, until 1890. The station was modernised in 1954 when the concourse was rebuilt. As the 1960s gave way to the 70s and main line passenger trains were withdrawn or rerouted, the concourse was given over to handling increasing amounts of parcels and is seen here during that transition on 2nd August, 1966. *(by courtesy of the Bradford Telegraph & Argus)*

Although only a short distance, it was a major undertaking and took two and a half years to complete because a deep, sharply curved cutting had to be dug down a 1 in 49 gradient. The line was opened in January, 1867 and the L&Y station was renamed Exchange two months later. Adolphus Street continued as a goods depot.

Situated at the foot of a 1 in 50 falling gradient from Bowling Tunnel, Drake Street opened in 1850 and originally consisted of just one island platform with tracks on each side. A new platform and extra waiting rooms were added to cater for the GN traffic but the station still had to be enlarged on a massive scale between 1885 and 1887.

The new Bradford Exchange was a magnificent structure with 10 platforms housed under a glazed roof of two 100ft-span wrought iron arches. In the centre of the station, they were supported by 18 Corinthian-style cast iron columns manufactured locally while at their outer ends the arches rested on corbels in the 40ft high masonry walls.

All the station offices were situated around the main concourse which had entrances via a main approach from Bridge Street, a subway and staircase from Hall Ings, and a side wall at the bottom of Drake Street.

After a lingering death lasting several years, it was replaced by the present Interchange station in 1973 and what remained was demolished soon after.

Notable among later lines to be built were the steeply-graded Laisterdyke–Shipley which although intended as a suburban line, provided a roundabout connection between Bradford's two separate rail networks, and the spectacular Queensbury lines which set up alternative routes to Keighley and Halifax.

The Laisterdyke–Shipley line was proposed in 1866 by two small companies – the Bradford, Eccleshill and Idle, and the Idle and Shipley. Both were soon swallowed up by the Great Northern and the line opened to freight in 1874 and to passengers a year later. Badly hit by bus competition, this route lost its regular passenger trains as early as 1931, although excursions continued until the early 1960s. The line stayed a useful cross-city freight link until 1964 after which only the Shipley–Idle section remained, surviving until October, 1968.

Work started on building the line to Thornton through Queensbury in 1874 but it

Bradford's north and south rail systems were destined never to be united and the nearest to a link between the two was the Shipley–Laisterdyke line through Idle. Although its full potential was never exploited in this way, it proved useful for cross-city freight until ceasing to be a through route in 1964. It was also used by special passenger trains such as this excursion seen passing Idle hauled by a pair of Black Fives in 1956. *(Peter Sunderland)*

was October, 1878 before the first passenger trains were running. This was because of a number of major engineering works, notably the 1,057 yard Clayton Tunnel and the 20 arch Thornton Viaduct across the Pinchbeck Valley on the approach to Thornton station. However, the most difficult job was the construction of a huge 104ft high embankment to carry the line across High Birks valley between Queensbury and Thornton.

The Halifax line proved equally difficult with a 2,501 yard tunnel having to be blasted through solid rock just outside Queensbury station. Mile for mile, the Queensbury lines were the costliest to build in the West Riding.

The last Bradford line to be built was the short-lived GNR link between Low Moor and Dudley Hill which opened in December, 1893 and prompted the introduction of a circular service from Leeds Central to Tingley, Batley, Dewsbury, Thornhill, Cleckheaton, Low Moor, Dudley Hill, Pudsey and back to Leeds Central – a distance of just under 30 miles which took 90 minutes.

By the turn of the century, Bradford's 300,000 population was being served by six major railway companies. Besides the GNR,

the Midland and the L&Y which had their own lines into the city, the Great Central, the North Eastern, and London and North Western enjoyed running rights or other arrangements. All but the GC had their own booking offices.

Competition was intense and, in 1874, the Midland introduced Britain's first Pullman service between Bradford and St Pancras. It lasted only two years, though, as the company decided to use the coaches on the newly-opened Settle–Carlisle line instead.

Another short-lived innovation was the LNWR's first and last sleeper train from London to Yorkshire which ran from Euston between January and June, 1906.

Main line passenger services continued to develop, however, and in the 1950s Bradford was served by no less than six named expresses, including two Pullman trains. All but two ran as portions from Exchange station and connected with the main Kings Cross trains at Leeds or Wakefield. The premier train was the Yorkshire Pullman, replaced on Sundays by a portion of the Harrogate Sunday Pullman. The West Riding ran to Kings Cross in the morning and returned in the evening, while a

Adolphus Street must have been one of the most grandiose goods sheds in the country, the 100ft-span arched roof originally covering the Great Northern Railway's first Bradford station. It soldiered on for 105 years as a goods depot, and was pictured on 25th June, 1957 with ferry vans on the right having brought perishable goods from the Continent and, left, what appear to be rolls of paper. *(by courtesy of the Bradford Telegraph & Argus)*

corresponding train from London was the White Rose. Also from Exchange was The South Yorkshireman to London Marylebone via Huddersfield, Sheffield and the Great Central main line. The one named train from Forster Square at this time was The Devonian to Paignton. All except the South Yorkshireman, which was rerouted to Kings Cross in 1961, lasted well into the 1960s, the Yorkshire Pullman and Devonian still running in 1993, albeit starting at Leeds.

It is now almost impossible to imagine just how much freight was generated by Bradford a century ago, yet today the city has no goods yards left, and the only regular freight is a weekly train serving a Shipley scrapyard.

Apart from the vast Adolphus Street complex, Bradford's main city goods yards included Drake Street (L&Y) which was replaced by the much larger Bridge Street depot in 1884. This closed in 1962 and the site is now occupied by the Bradford Interchange bus station.

The Midland's yard was in Valley Road which in August, 1984 became the last city goods depot to close.

Laisterdyke, in the industrial south east of the city, had goods yards at Planetrees and Quarry Gap, while about a mile west of the city centre was City Road.

This GN yard opened in 1876 and occupied a large site boasting six miles of sidings. It closed in August, 1972 and 20 years later the site was occupied by Europe's biggest single-storey warehouse belonging to Grattan's mail order company. The GN also had its own goods depot in L&Y territory at Low Moor, served by the branch from Dudley Hill, but it closed with the branch in 1917.

On the GN side, a small marshalling yard was developed at Quarry Gap where trains arriving in Bradford were broken up and wagons formed into trips to the various depots and vice-versa. These included workings for City Road and beyond, and via Idle to the GN's terminus at Shipley Windhill.

In addition, most suburban stations such as Manchester Road, Horton Park, Eccleshill, Manningham and Frizinghall, all had their own goods and coal yards, making Bradford a seething mass of freight activity.

The three companies directly serving Bradford each had their own locomotive depots too. The Midland's consisted of one of its standard roundhouses situated amid the extensive sidings at Manningham, the GN's straight shed and heavy repair shop were alongside the St Dunstan's–Laisterdyke line at Bowling, while the L&Y had its own operations centre at Low Moor which included a large straight shed, carriage sidings and goods yard. The GN carriage sidings were at St Dunstan's while the Midland's were on the east and west sides of the lines approaching Forster Square.

The post-war decline of Bradford's railways was so rapid as to be almost beyond belief with most of the damage being done in the 1951-66 period.

The Laisterdyke–Shipley passenger service, and the Low Moor–Dudley Hill line, were early casualties but the biggest loss came on 23rd May, 1955 when the Queensbury lines passenger services were withdrawn. Goods traffic over certain portions lasted another 10 years.

All services over the Pudsey loop were axed by Dr Beeching in 1964, as were local trains to Wakefield via Dewsbury. Local services between Forster Square and Leeds went on 22nd March, 1965 and passenger trains to Wakefield via Morley, notably the Bradford portions of Kings Cross expresses, were rerouted via Leeds in July, 1966. Local services to Huddersfield and beyond via Low Moor were axed on 14th June, 1965, the remaining Stockport service following on 5th November, 1966. During the 1950s and 60s most suburban stations around Bradford were closed but more significantly the city lost most of its long-distance expresses, condemning it to become a railway backwater.

As the 1960s gave way to the 70s, Bradford was left with only local services from Forster Square to Ilkley and Keighley, and from Exchange to Leeds, Manchester, Southport and Blackpool, plus a smattering of InterCity trains from Exchange.

Intervention by the West Yorkshire Passenger Transport Executive which under Section 20 of the 1968 Transport Act began financially supporting local passenger services in 1976, saved what was left of the system, as did specific acts of support by the City Council.

In the late 1980s it looked as though the tide might be turning. The threatened InterCity link with London was saved and switched to Forster Square while Frizinghall station, closed in 1965, was reopened.

By the end of 1994 all routes out of Forster Square will have been electrified and the local service to Leeds via Shipley reinstated while British Rail has promised six electric InterCity trains a day to Kings Cross. It remains to be seen, however, whether any future private operator will honour this pledge.

At the same, time signalling on Bradford's north side is being fully modernised, bringing the whole of Airedale and Wharfedale under the control of the power box at Leeds and eliminating the remaining Midland Railway signal boxes, including those at Shipley.

But Bradford will always be at a disadvantage so long as it remains tethered to two dead end branch lines. The closest it ever came to having a vital link across the city was a scheme by the Midland Railway which almost achieved fruition early this century but the company got cold feet and delayed the project so long that the first world war intervened. It formally abandoned the plan in 1919 and although the issue has been raised from time to time since, it seems unlikely now that anything will ever be done.

In true Bradford tradition, we have to make the best of a bad job – but at least the future of our surviving lines and stations now seems brighter than for many years – privatisation permitting!

The approach to Bradford Exchange on Saturday 10th July, 1965 with Fairburn tanks Nos.42141 and 42074 pausing between duties. In the background are the single-storey Bridge Street goods depot and multi-storey wool warehouse, closed in 1962 and cleared of all track. This whole area is today occupied by the huge transport interchange which opened to rail traffic in 1973 but was not fully completed until 1977. *(Brian Myland)*

THE POWER OF BRADFORD

There was an amazing variety of motive power around Bradford as the 1950s dawned with the city's three locomotive depots all retaining their own company lineage.

This soon changed in 1954 when Bowling shed, later known as Hammerton Street, became home to the very first of the diesel multiple units that were to oust steam and become the backbone of suburban and rural passenger services throughout Britain for the next 40 years.

New diesel facilities were provided and the depot's remaining steam locomotives transferred to Low Moor from January, 1958. These included B1 4-6-0s, J39 and J6 0-6-0s, and J50 0-6-0Ts. The N1 0-6-2Ts – stalwarts of the Queensbury line passenger service – had been transferred away in 1957 after ending their days on Kings Cross portions to and from Wakefield.

Manningham shed in the late 1950s was home to about a dozen different steam types, including a trio of Compound 4-4-0s whose regular duties included the Forster Square–Morecambe 'Residential'. This carried wool magnates home to the Lancashire resort – once dubbed 'Bradford-by-the-Sea' because of the numerous Bradfordians who retired there – after a day's business in the West Riding. It combined at Skipton with another portion from Leeds.

Other locos on Manningham's books included ex-LMS Class 3 and Ivatt Class 2 2-6-2Ts, and the Fairburn 2-6-4Ts which were a familiar sight to the end. In late LMS days, Stanier three-cylinder 2-6-4Ts Nos.2522/4/5 spent a short time at Manningham before going back to their native London, Tilbury and Southend line. Despite being of Midland origin, the shed also had a number of L&Y Radial tanks with 10 there in 1950 for use on both local and express passenger trains. Nos.50636 and 50795 survived into the late 1950s with 50795 the last to go, withdrawn in December,1959.

Manningham freight types included Crab 2-6-0s, 3F and 4F 0-6-0s and a few Jinty 0-6-0Ts. In the late 1940s, it also turned out Midland 0-4-4T No.1413 as Forster Square station pilot.

There was less variety in the 1960s but passenger, freight and parcels workings into Forster Square often brought unusual visitors to Manningham for servicing alongside more regular interlopers like Britannia and Clan Pacifics from Carlisle.

One of the rarest I can recall was V2 2-6-2 No.60885 which appeared on 21st October, 1964,

Pure Bradford – The South Yorkshireman, Low Moor pet Jubilee *Victoria* and, in the background, the city's evening newspaper, the Telegraph and Argus – not to mention the rain.
The South Yorkshireman to London Marylebone typified the diversity of long-distance expresses that once served the city. This train ran once a day in each direction but back in 1946 the LNER ran two trains to Marylebone and four back. In this picture only the headboard is genuine, however. It was in fact taken on 5th September, 1965, four years after the South Yorkshireman was switched to Kings Cross and shows *Victoria* setting off with a railtour to Crewe organised by the Halifax Railfans. (*Barry Mounsey*)

In steam days, Liverpool Exchange–Leeds/Bradford trains travelling over the L&Y main line, divided at Low Moor, one portion continuing to Bradford and the other taking the Bowling Junction–Laisterdyke line direct to Leeds. The reverse procedure was followed by trains travelling the opposite way, one of which is seen on 15th April, 1961 with Liverpool Bank Hall Standard Class 4 4-6-0 No.75047 ready for departure. (*Peter Rose*)

This operation ended when the Calder Valley DMUs replaced steam in January, 1962, all trains then running instead via Bradford Exchange.

later working the 19.45 Bradford Valley–Carlisle goods. Darlington K1 2-6-0 No.62001 was another 1964 visitor, having brought a parcels train in from Leeds, while in the spring of 1966 A2 Pacific No.60532 *Blue Peter* arrived with empty stock from Dundee. That all ended at midnight on 29th April, 1967 when Manningham closed, leaving Low Moor as Bradford's last steam shed.

Dating from 1866, Low Moor was built to replace a small shed at Drake Street. Enlarged to 12 roads in 1890, its allocation of engines once stood at 123. Half the shed was pulled down just before the second world war but the rest was rebuilt afterwards and remained largely unaltered until closure.

Passenger engines always predominated. Among Low Moor's pre-war allocation was a small stud of Compound 4-4-0s, including 1199 which was a local stalwart from 1930 to 1946.

Transfer of Bowling's steam allocation in 1958 gave Low Moor a distinctly LNER flavour which it never lost. For a short time in 1961 it borrowed a pair of K3 2-6-0s from Ardsley for use on Blackpool trains while two years earlier it hosted K1s 62047 and 62065 for an equally brief period. December, 1961 saw the transfer of four Thompson L1 2-6-4Ts from Ardsley to Low Moor. Intended to replace the J50s they were found to be unsuitable and rarely ventured out.

In September, 1961, Royal Scots Nos. 46109/113/117/130 and 145 were sent to Low Moor after being displaced from Leeds Holbeck by diesels. They were put to work on freight during the week, for which they were totally unsuitable, and on Blackpool trains via Copy Pit on Saturdays, on which they performed admirably.

No.46109 spent most of its time at Crewe Works while 46113/117/145 were loaned to Mirfield in January, 1962. By June all five had returned to Holbeck and Low Moor received Jubilees 45565 *Victoria* and 45694 *Bellerophon* instead.

Low Moor developed a close association with the B1s and was the last shed in the country to operate them with 61030 *Nyala*, 61306 and 61337 surviving to the end of Bradford steam.

The B1s were rostered for a wide variety of work, ranging from the Yorkshire Pullman and summer Saturday seaside excursions to humble pick-up freights.

During August, 1964 long-serving No.61189 *Sir William Gray* was used on weekday tracklifting trains between Thornton and Cullingworth on the GN Keighley line while turning out every Saturday for its regular seaside passenger turns.

Although mainly a passenger depot, Low Moor did have some heavy goods engines, notably the WD 2-8-0s which were used on a wide variety of trip freight and shunt duties. Regular workings included the Laisterdyke to Thornton and Cullingworth shunts with 90711 – a Low Moor engine from June, 1958 until withdrawal in January, 1967 – being a regular on what were often heavy trains.

The end for Low Moor came on 2nd October, 1967 when Black Five 45208 was the last loco in steam. A few dead engines remained dumped at the back of the shed until Christmas when they were dragged off to Wakefield pending sale for scrap.

The Airedale line through Shipley was always interesting and even as late as 1966 a good variety of engines could be expected. The arrival of Peak, BR Sulzer Type 2 (Class 24 and 25) and Brush Type 4 diesels at Leeds in the early 1960s made inroads into steam but it continued to make frequent forays out of Forster Square with Class 1 passenger duties.

The Bradford–Morecambe 'Resi' often turned up a Lancaster Patriot in 1961/2 while Britannias continued to stand in for the Peaks on Leeds–Glasgow expresses. Top line duties such as the Bradford–Penzance Cornishman and the Devonian also had regular steam haulage as far as Leeds until 1967.

By the middle of 1963, Bradford–Morecambe and Leeds–Carnforth workings were mainly in the hands of Black Fives and Jubilees although Crab and Ivatt 4 2-6-0s appeared from time to time. Diesels also took frequent turns on the Morecambe trains from 1963.

Main line steam passenger workings out of Forster Square in 1964 included the 14.00 to Sheffield, and the 21.30 St Pancras as far as Leeds – a regular steam turn using a loco which arrived earlier on the evening stopping service from Carlisle.

A favourite with local enthusiasts was the 15.40 Forster Square to Carlisle stopper which was rostered for a Carlisle Kingmoor engine. During 1965, it produced Britannias, Black Fives, Jubilees or one of the dwindling number of Clans.

Across at Exchange, steam still dominated the London portions to and from Wakefield and the one daily working which ran via Halifax and Huddersfield. On a summer Saturday in 1965, no less than eight steam-hauled trains were to be seen leaving Exchange between 07.14 and 09.30 with the 07.14 Yarmouth, 08.02 Skegness and 08.30 Cleethorpes being double-headed.

Steam continued on seaside trains from Bradford in 1966 but 5th November saw the last Stockport service hauled by Fairburn tank No.42116. On the same day, Low Moor stablemate 42233 was on the 15.05 to Kings Cross, B1 No.61013 *Topi* the 21.25 Kings Cross, and Stanier tank 42574 the 22.00 Huddersfield mail.

By the start of 1967, Bradford was a mecca for steam fans with Fairburn and Stanier tanks, Black Fives and occasional B1s still working daily on Leeds–Bradford passenger trains, sometimes in tandem with Holbeck Class 24 or 25 diesels.

In summer, 1967, the last for steam on the seaside specials, the highlight of the week was the Saturday race up the 1 in 50 gradient to Mill Lane by the 08.20 Bridlington and Skegness trains. The Bridlington train was by then the longest regular out and back working for a steam crew in the country.

The inevitable end came on Sunday 1st October when Fairburn No.42152 had the honour of working the last steam-hauled Bradford–Leeds passenger train. The day before, Bradford Exchange saw the last B1 working when 61306 hauled the Huddersfield mail before being withdrawn.

Steam continued to skirt the city on freights through Shipley though. Its last stand in Airedale came in the shape of the big 9F 2-10-0s – often 92167 – piloting a Class 25 diesel on the daily Heysham–Leeds oil tanks. This interesting combination continued until early summer, 1968, and was the last steam working I ever saw in the Bradford area.

Hammerton Street was by this time noted for its Class 110 DMUs, specially built in 1961 to replace steam on Liverpool trains via the Calder Valley, and its 204hp (Class 03 and 04)) and 350hp (Class 08) diesel shunters. It also had a batch of Hunslet Class 05 shunters in 1966 but they were little used. The axe fell on Hammerton Street in May, 1984 and the buildings were demolished in 1991.

Early diesel traction – itself now history – also saw service in the Bradford area with Peaks, Deltics, English Electric Type 4s (Class 40s) and the Sulzer Type 2s all daily visitors.

In the late 1950s, the Airedale line echoed to the sound of the ill-fated Metrovick Co-Bos on the London–Glasgow Condor express freight, while in 1963 the Idle branch was used to test a brand new Clayton centre-cab Type 1 (Class 17).

The Deltic-shaped Class 50 prototype DP2 worked regularly to Exchange station on the White Rose before its sad and untimely demise in a serious crash north of York on 31st July, 1967.

Ironically, by the 1990s there was again more steam variety in Bradford than diesel. The only diesel locomotives to regularly visit the city were Class 47s on remaining parcels trains from the Interchange but the steam-hauled legs of Kings Cross–Carlisle excursions from Forster Square have seen everything from ex-LMS Stanier Pacifics and the BR Standard Class 8P *Duke of Gloucester* to ex-LNER A2, A3 and A4 Pacifics, Jubilees and even a BR Standard 2-6-4T – all preserved of course.

Back in the 1960s this scene at Bradford Exchange would barely have warrented a second glance, so commonplace were the Fairburn 2-6-4Ts. Nearly 30 years later, however, 42269 and 42689 make a stirring sight as they boil up in platforms 8 and 9 on 30th April, 1966. (*Brian Myland*)

BRADFORD NORTH

Forster Square was an important terminus, sending passenger trains to London, the Midlands, the West Country and the North. In summer, 1957, besides local trains to Leeds City, Ilkley and Skipton both via Ilkley and Keighley, there were four trains a day to St Pancras, three to Morecambe, two to Bristol and one each to Bournemouth, Newcastle, Scarborough, Paignton, Hull, Sheffield, Derby, Garsdale, Carlisle and Heysham Harbour.

Top: One of those departures was the 15.40 stopping train to Carlisle, ready to leave platform 6 on 25th March, 1964 with grimy Britannia Pacific No.70008 *Black Prince* at the head. (*Michael Leahy*)

The entrance to Forster Square station was not particularly impressive but the Midland Hotel (centre) and the Valley Road goods offices in the right of the bottom picture added a fair degree of grandeur.

The offices were demolished in 1975 but the hotel, famous for being the place where actor and impressario Sir Henry Irving died in 1905, was still standing and part occupied by a restaurant in 1993. (*by courtesy of British Rail*)

Parcels traffic continued to flourish after Forster Square lost its main line passenger trains, thanks to the orders despatched by Bradford mail order houses Grattan and Empire Stores. Most of the platforms were given over to parcels trains which left every night for destinations all over the country, and the spacious concourse adapted as a mechanised parcels depot handling up to 40,000 packages a day.

But in the late 1970s the traffic declined as the mail order firms switched to road and increasing numbers of discount stores and hypermarkets took a large chunk of their market. The final death knell came in 1980 when BR closed its Collection and Delivery parcels service.

Top: Looking towards the hotel, which had an entrance directly from the concourse, on 19th December, 1969 with a battery-powered tractor and a line of BRUTE containers for loading straight on to the train. (*by courtesy of British Rail*)

Centre: During modernisation in 1954 Forster Square's overall roof was replaced by canopies, seen to good effect on 28th December, 1987 when only platforms one and two remained in use for local trains. (*Malcolm Roughley*)

Bottom: Happier times. Fireman Sedgewick of Leeds Holbeck prepares the headlamps on Jubilee 4-6-0 No.45608 *Gibraltar* before taking out the 6.15pm to Leeds City on 13th July, 1961. (*Roy Wood*)

Above: Enthusiasts savour the atmosphere of steam as now-preserved Holbeck Jubilee No.45593 *Kolhapur* prepares for departure with a railtour to Carlisle on 30th April, 1966. (*Brian Myland*) By 1993 Forster Square was again seeing steam specials to and from Carlisle but this could be short-lived as electrification in 1994 may spell the end of steam working from the city.

Below: Looking north from Forster Square on 7th February, 1964 as Britannia Pacific No.70002 *Geoffrey Chaucer* leaves platform 6 with the 15.40 to Carlisle. The West carriage sidings – site of the new station opened in June, 1990 – are on the left. (*Brian Myland*) This view shows how extensive the railway once was but after the new station opened the whole area was cleared to make room for a multi-million pound shopping and leisure complex of which the new station was to be a part. The plans fell through and in 1992 the old station was demolished and turned into a car park until new development plans emerge.

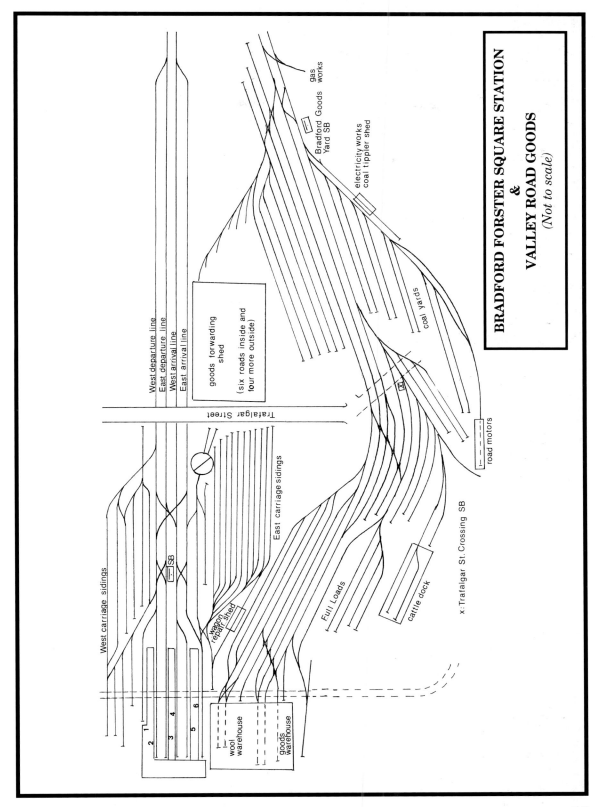

BRADFORD FORSTER SQUARE STATION
&
VALLEY ROAD GOODS
(Not to scale)

Top: The Devonian brought Western Region chocolate and cream coaches such as BR Mk1 BSK No.W34956, to workaday Bradford, reminding a lucky few of sunshine holidays on England's Riviera. Waiting to take the express to Leeds City on the first leg of its journey on 15th March, 1961 was Holbeck's Fowler 2-6-4T No.42409. (*Roy Wood*)

Centre: Forster Square carriage sidings survived well into the 1980s, as did much of the station layout. They were last used for storing withdrawn electric trains from London's Great Eastern suburban lines during their journey to the scrapyard. These Class 306 units were seen there on 4th February, 1984. More were stored in the station itself. (*Stephen Chapman*)

Bottom: This general view of the station throat on 17th August, 1961 is full of Midland Railway character with lower-quadrant signals, a gas lamp and even a MR clerestory van in the sidings on the right. (*Peter Rose*) Comparison with the picture on page 14 shows that signalling was modernised between 1961 and 1964. Further rationalisation in 1984 eliminated the signal box and brought control of this once important terminus under Bradford Junction box at Shipley.

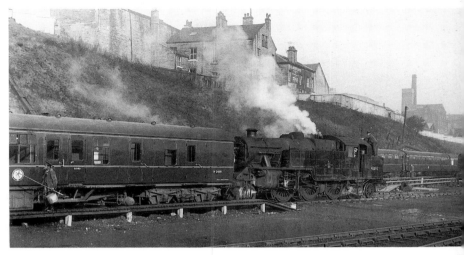

Top: Forster Square West carriage sidings with Manningham's Fairburn 2-6-4T No.42093 on 30th April, 1966. (*Brian Myland*)

Centre: A wintry view of the West carriage sidings looking towards the station with Ivatt Class 4 2-6-0 No.43016 manouvring stock. (*Michael Leahy*) **The East carriage sidings are on the extreme left along with the Valley Road goods complex.**

Bottom: On 5th August, 1967 Holbeck Jubilee No.45697 *Achilles* **was on menial work at East carriage sidings while sisters 45562** *Alberta* **and 45593** *Kolhapur* **were on morning and afternoon Leeds–Carlisle expresses respectively. Later that afternoon 45697 worked the Bradford–Heysham parcels.** (*Barry Mounsey*)

Above: Ivatt Class 4 2-6-0 No.43113 of Lancaster Green Ayre brings the 9.5am from Leeds City beneath the stubby upper quadrant signals designed to give drivers of approaching trains a clear view beneath Trafalgar Street bridge through which it has just passed. The date is 11th September, 1961 and Holbeck Black Five No.44857 is on the right. (*Roy Wood*)

Below: One of the great thrills of the steam age was to see a big engine on the turntable. It was all coming to an end on 29th April, 1967 when Black Five No.44824 was being serviced prior to turning on the Forster Square turntable during preparation for working the last steam Devonian. (*Michael Leahy*)

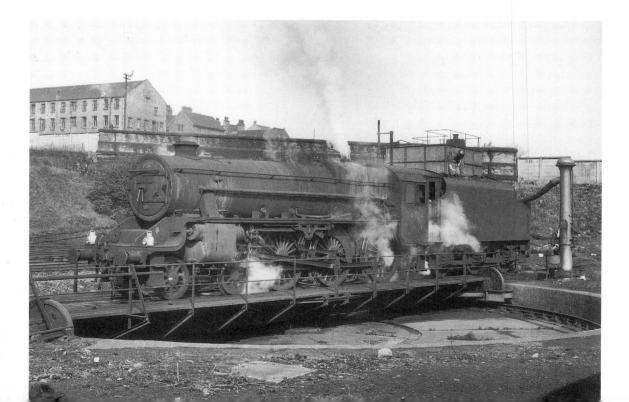

Above: The location of this picture will be familiar to enginemen who worked into Forster Square. Manningham's stalwart 4F No.44216 was photographed on 15th March, 1961 from the footplate of Fowler 2-6-4T No.42409 while it was on the turntable. The 4F's fireman appears to be moving coal forward on the tender. The engine is facing Bradford which suggests it still needs to be turned before taking its train. (*Roy Wood*)

Peter Rose was a fireman at Leeds Holbeck until 1959 and regularly worked steam into Forster Square. "Normally, we would run straight into platform 6. Then the shunt engine, usually 41265 or 66, came on and took the stock away and we would back our engine straight onto the turntable road, water and turn. We then backed out again, went forward to the crossover beyond the signal box, and reversed onto our return train in one of the departure side platforms."

Below: Although the Midland route into Bradford had its own motive power depot at Manningham, many trains were worked by engines from Leeds Holbeck. Here, one of Holbeck's Black Fives with Caprotti valve gear, Timken roller bearings and double chimney, No.44756, storms out of the city with the 10.10am to St Pancras on a very frosty March, 1963 morning. (*Michael Leahy*)

North side freight was concentrated on the Bradford Valley complex to the east and north of Forster Square station. It comprised the large three-storey goods and wool warehouse next to the station, the Trafalgar Street freight forwarding shed, full loads sidings, a wagon repair shed, sorting sidings, coal yard and cattle dock.

Above: Trafalgar was a separate depot until October, 1962 when it was merged with Valley Road. It was used entirely for the despatch of freight sundries (all manner of part wagonloads) and had been handed over to the road-orientated National Carriers Ltd by the start of the 1970s. After that the decline was quick as traffic switched to road.

At one time, express freight trains ran direct from Bradford Valley to destinations all over the country. In April, 1963 they included the 6.45pm to Dock Junction (London), the 6.55pm Low Moor via Laisterdyke, and the 7.15 for Westerleigh (Bristol). There were also regular trips to West Riding marshalling yards which before long included the 7.25pm to Healey Mills, seen being prepared for departure behind Manchester Newton Heath 9F 2-10-0 No.92208 on 26th June, 1964.

Below: Skipton-based 4F 0-6-0 No.44041 brings a long train into Bradford Valley past the Corporation electricity generating works during the big freeze on 16th February, 1963. (*both Michael Leahy*)

During the 1960s the International Harvesters factory at Idle sent large numbers of tractors by rail for export. Many went to Dunkirk and left on the 6.45pm Bradford Valley to Dock Junction. Unfortunately, thieves used to steal the toolboxes en route and the railway had to pay compensation which ate up all the profit.

Top: Special working 4X05 leaves Bradford Valley behind Black Five No.45204 while (centre) on 2nd July, 1964 this formidable train, hauled by Sulzer Type 2 diesel No. D7580, conveyed 53 tyreless tractors for Dunkirk. (*both Michael Leahy*)

Below: The top floor of Valley Road wool warehouse on 6th May, 1959. (*by courtesy of British Rail*) A two-road section nearest the station was dedicated to wool while the other three-road portion was for general goods. Bonded goods and full loads, including more wool, were handled in the yard outside.

Reduced to a public delivery siding, Bradford Valley closed on 6th August, 1984 when remaining full loads traffic was transferred to Leeds Whitehall Road and Dewsbury Railway Street. The last trip working ran on 3rd August behind Class 31 diesel No.31288.

September, 1958: Manningham Compound 4-4-0s, usually 41063 or 41163, regularly work the 8.21am Skipton to Liverpool Exchange, a through train from Forster Square. The engine then works the 1.30pm Liverpool Exchange to Preston.

7.7.59: K1 2-6-0 No.62065 and Ivatt 2-6-2T No. 41253 (both of Low Moor) double-head the 2.57pm Penistone stopping train out of Bradford Exchange.

March, 1959: Low Moor's L&Y 0-6-0ST, No.51404, is withdrawn.

11.6.60: A3 4-6-2 No.60038 *Firdaussi* passes through Shipley with the Up Thames–Clyde Express.

22.7.60: New England-based A2 4-6-2 No.60533 *Happy Knight* is seen standing light engine on the Bingley Jn–Bradford Jn curve at Shipley.

Above: The weather had improved but the smoke effects were nearly as good as on page 19 when Fairburn tank No.42188 made a fine show passing Trafalgar goods with the 8.50am to St Pancras. (*Michael Leahy*) Back in 1946, Bradford had as many as 10 direct trains each weekday to St Pancras, Kings Cross or Marylebone. In 1993 the city had just one, the 07.04 from Forster Square to Kings Cross, and two from Kings Cross at 15.50 and 18.10.

Below: A pure Midland scene at Manningham station where 2P 4-4-0 No.40518 is calling while en-route to Forster Square with a stopping train on 21st July, 1955. The hut on the left was used as a clubroom by the Bradford Railway Circle whose members have kindly assisted with this book. Manningham engine shed is on the right. (*G.H.Butland*)

Above: Another vintage view of Manningham station, this time with Stanier Class 3 2-6-2T No.40120 calling there on 14th July, 1955. In summer, 1957 Manningham was served by nine trains to Skipton, eight to Leeds City, three to Ilkley and one each to Morecambe, Carlisle, and Skipton via Ilkley. The station closed on 22nd March, 1965 when the local service to Leeds was withdrawn. (*G.H. Butland*)

Below: On Saturdays during early 1965 Carlisle Royal Scots and rebuilt Patriots, displaced from more important work, regularly appeared on the 15.40 Forster Square to Carlisle stopper. Here, No.46115 *Scots Guardsman* calls at Manningham. (*Barry Mounsey*)

Manningham motive power depot was coded 20E in the BR London Midland Region Leeds district until 1956 when the whole district was transferred to the North Eastern Region and it became 55F. The depot closed completely on 29th April, 1967 and the site is now occupied by an industrial estate.
Above: A variety of ex-LMS engines cluster round the Manningham roundhouse turntable. They are, from left: Fairburn 2-6-4T No 42141, Ivatt Class 2 2-6-2T No.41266, Hughes-Fowler Crab 2-6-0 No.42774 and an 8F 2-8-0. (*Michael Leahy*)

LOCOMOTIVES ALLOCATED TO MANNINGHAM
(Including locos sub-shedded at Keighley)
Summer,1950

Fowler 3P 2-6-2T: 40069; Midland 2P 4-4-0: 40455/89; LMS 2P 4-4-0: 40567; Midland Compound 4-4-0: 41004; LMS Compound 4-4-0: 41067/9/80/1197; Ivatt 2MT 2-6-2T: 41265/6; Fairburn 4MT 2-6-4T:42146/682/5; Fowler 4MT 2-6-4T: 42377/80; 5P5F 2-6-0: 42762; Johnson 3F 0-6-0: 43178/351/742/70; LMS 4F 0-6-0: 44216/400/555/70; Ivatt 2MT 2-6-0: 46452/3; Midland 3F 0-6-0T: 47222/55; LMS 3F 0-6-0T: 47419; L&Y 2P 2-4-2T: 50623/30/3/4/6/71/81/9/714/95/842; Midland 1P 0-4-4T: 58069/70; Midland 2F 0-6-0:58154. Total 44.

July, 1962

350hp diesel shunter: D3457/656/7/8; Ivatt 2MT 2-6-2T: 41266/73; Fairburn 4MT 2-6-4T: 42072/93/2139/89; 5P5F 2-6-0:42774/89; Ivatt 4MT 2-6-0:43016/30/74; 3F 0-6-0: 43586; 4F 0-6-0:44039/55/97/216/400. Total 21.

November,1966

204hp diesel shunter: D2044/71/161; Fairburn 4MT 2-6-4T: 42072/93/138/52/89; Ivatt 4MT 2-6-0: 43044/50/1/4/99/117. Total 14.

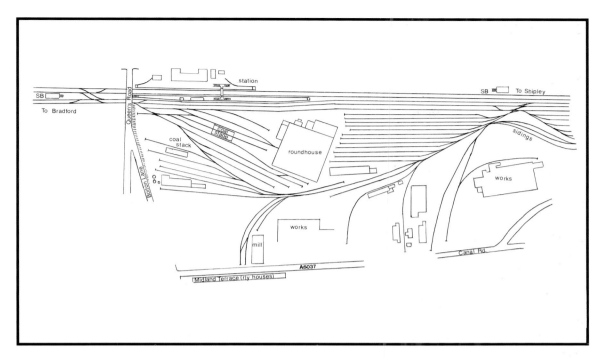

Above: Manningham MPD and station in 1959 (*Not to scale*).
Below: A general view of the depot yard in 1961 with Midland 3F 0-6-0 No.43681 coming off shed. The roundhouse is on the left and the coal stack with neatly whitewashed border in the centre. On the right is Ivatt Class 2 2-6-2T No.41325, push-pull fitted for working the Worth Valley branch. (*Michael Leahy*)

Manningham mixture:
Top: 4F 0-6-0 No.44400 takes water next to the coaling stage in the early 1960s. One of the cranes which lifted tubs of coal onto locomotive tenders can be seen just inside. The modern chimney in the background forms part of a metal treatment works which was still in business 30 years later.

Bottom: Reposing inside the roundhouse with one of Manningham's BR 204hp diesel shunters in the mid-1960s were Fairburn 2-6-4Ts 42052 and 42072. (*both Michael Leahy*)

Centre: Awaiting its fate on 11th April 1954 but still maintaining a smart outward appearance, was Holbeck ex-LMS Compound 4-4-0 No.41103. The pile of small coal in the foreground was probably cleaned out of the tenders or bunkers of condemned engines, while the wall was made of briquettes. These were made from poor coal and would not burn well if fired whole and did not produce much heat when broken up so the wall was probably considered the best use for them. (*Brian Myland*)

Right: Stourton 4F No.44570 brings a mineral train towards Bradford, behind Manningham station and past the engine shed in 1961. (*Michael Leahy*)

Left: BR Standard 3MT 2-6-0 No.77012 was a well-known York engine and was indeed one of the last steam locomotives working from that shed when it closed to steam in June, 1967. For a time, though, it was allocated to Manningham and is seen in almost pristine condition inside the round-house on 25th May, 1965. (*D. Butterfield*)

Right: Having its fire cleaned on the Manningham ash pit on 15th March, 1963 was Carlisle King-moor rebuilt Patriot 4-6-0 No.45535 *Sir Herbert Walker KCB*. (*Roy Wood*)

Brian Whitaker started work at Frizinghall wool warehouse in 1958, working a 44-hour week for seven pounds and seven shillings.

"We handled bales of wool and mohair, bags of soda ash from ICI Burn Naze or Northwich, and newsprint for the Telegraph and Argus. In 16 cwt rolls from Bowaters, Ellesmere Port, newsprint was the heaviest item and was unloaded using a creaky old overhead crane in 'A' room at the north end of the building. Wool and mohair came from Hull, Goole, Liverpool, Southampton, and London Poplar Docks from where we once aquired a cat in a 12 ton box van.

Arriving goods were sometimes stored for customers until required. We had Scammell Scarab 6-ton three wheelers, known as 'cobs', for deliveries. Woolcombers Ltd. and C.W. & N. Roe were among firms collecting their own along with Raspins woolcombers who sent a horse dray for soda ash.

"The mohair was stored for Kassapian & Sons whose staff came to the warehouse to weigh and check the bags on arrival.

"Our basic staff consisted of stationmaster, chief clerk, two clerks, foreman, three checkers, three cranemen, five or six goods porters and two motor drivers. Many relief staff were used at busy times.

"We also handled bottles for the United Glass Bottle company. They varied from miniature spirit bottles through beer and milk to pint spirit bottles, the latter for E.T. Walls at Keighley who were well known rum blenders."

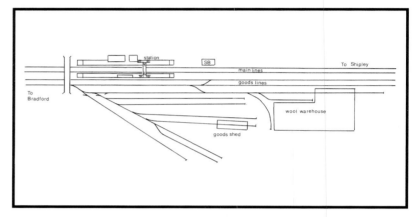

Top: Next station going out of Bradford was Frizinghall, pictured being passed by a Metro-Cammell DMU to Forster Square on 23rd June, 1967. This station also closed on 22nd March, 1965 but a new unstaffed halt was opened there by West Yorkshire PTE in 1987. (*by courtesy of the Bradford Telegraph & Argus*)

Above: Frizinghall station and goods yard in the early 1960s. The yard included two coal roads used by Barron's coal merchants. Reduced to a public delivery siding, it closed on 6th July, 1970.

Below: Frizinghall wool warehouse, seen from the street on 6th May, 1959. The building was formally Hodgson's loom works, believed to have ceased trading about 1934 and handed over to the LMS in lieu of debts. (*by courtesy of British Rail*)

In 1993 the only freight traffic left in the Bradford area was scrap metal from Crossley-Evans who occupied the site of Shipley goods yard. On 18th July, 1961 the yard was still fulfilling its original purpose and being shunted (top) by 3F 0-6-0 No.43586. (*Peter Rose*)

Centre: Steam was still shunting there in 1982 long after Crossley's had taken over the site. This time it was their own shunter, 0-4-0ST *Harry*, built by Andrew Barclay in 1924. A case of preservation in reverse, *Harry*, then called *Chemicals* was aquired from the Yorkshire Dales Railway in 1975, subsequently overhauled and repainted from black to blue. Not long after this picture was taken, *Harry* returned to preservation after being replaced by a 1969-built Hunslet diesel. Over the years, Crossley's had four other diesels, all 4-wheel shunters built between 1940 and 1959 by Ruston and Hornsby and two were still to be found at the end of a siding in 1993. (*Alan Whitaker*)

Bottom: Although taken as recently as 1st October, 1992, this view of Class 37 No.37506 *British Steel Skinningrove* passing Bradford Junction is already just a memory. A reorganisation by British Rail of its Trainload Metals operation in 1993 saw this Tuesdays and Thursdays trip working from Crossley-Evans rescheduled to run once a week as a longer train hauled by a more powerful Class 56. The Midland Railway signal box and semaphores were due to be swept away during 1994 by resignalling associated with electrification. (*Stephen Chapman*)

Top: The Gresley GNR Class N1 0-6-2Ts did sterling work on local passenger trains around Bradford until being made redundant by diesels and closures. Here, No.69430 of Leeds Copley Hill shed, ventures onto Midland metals in April, 1953 while turning on the Shipley triangle after bringing a railtour over the Idle branch to Windhill station. The loco is seen passing through platform one between Bradford and Bingley junctions. In 1993, only the right hand track remained, the platform long since denuded of its canopy. Platform one had been trackless for years but only lost its canopy in early 1993. (*D. Ibbotson*)

Centre: Britannia Pacific No.70003 *John Bunyan* leaves platform one and passes Bingley Junction signal box on 30th June, 1964 with the 15.40 to Carlisle. (*Brian Myland*)

Bottom: Shipley was a 'V'-shaped station and the main lines between Leeds and Bingley junctions on which Black Five No.44986 is travelling with a Down express goods on 30th June, 1964, had no platforms until recent times. The engineers' sidings were removed to make room for the first of the new platforms and a car park in 1979. (*Brian Myland*)

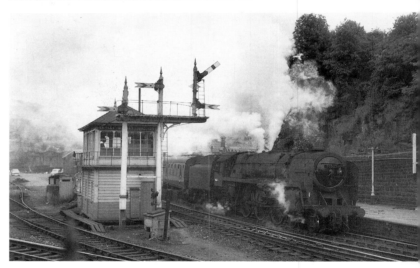

Loaded diesel multiple units booked to reverse direction at Shipley may be propelled from platform 2 or 4 to the Down Passenger line at Bradford Junction box. Drivers of such trains will not be verbally advised by the signalman and the Home signal concerned will be used for the movement. The tail lamp ... will not be transferred to the opposite end until the crossing movement has been made and the train has come to a stand at either platform 1 or 3.

Passenger trains (other than DMUs with tail traffic) and parcels trains may be propelled at Bingley Junction, from the Down Main to platform 1. In the case of parcels trains consisting of DMUs with tail traffic, the guard must ride in the leading driving compartment and the movement must be supervised by the person in charge of Shipley station.
Eastern Region Northern Area Sectional Appendix, 1968.

Above: Another view of the 15.40 Forster Square to Carlisle at Bingley Junction, this time headed by Royal Scot No.46152 *The King's Dragoon Guardsman* on 3rd April, 1965. Following reduction of the service between Bradford and Skipton, Leeds–Skipton trains, by then all DMUs, served Shipley by manoevring round the triangle. This continued until May, 1979 when a platform was added to the Down side of the main line, although Skipton to Leeds trains still had to cross over to reach this platform until another was opened on the Up side in 1992.

Below: The first diesel multiple units on BR were used on services out of Bradford from 1954. They were 2-car trains built at Derby Works similar to the Carlisle-based set seen being hauled west past Shipley Leeds Junction at the back of a parcels train on 3rd April, 1965. It was probably returning from overhaul at Derby and the rear vehicle, M79609, has bars on the opening windows, indicating that it worked the Cumbrian Coast where clearances were tight. (*both Brian Myland*)

BRADFORD SOUTH

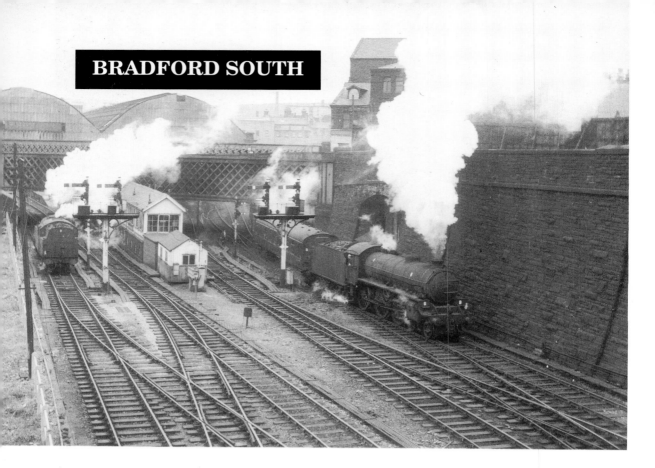

Above: A scene which many readers will remember well from the final years of steam at Bradford Exchange, and one which illustrates the rich mix of LMS/LNER motive power there. A B1 4-6-0 shunts coaches into the carriage sidings on the station's east side as a Fairburn 2-6-4T backs out of the station after working an incoming train. (*Peter Sunderland*)

Left: This modest entrance hardly seemed appropriate for the magnificent trainshed roof of Exchange station. Within a few years of this picture being taken on 8th May, 1968 the whole lot had gone, replaced by the Interchange. The buildings being demolished on the left were offices belonging to a wool company. (*by courtesy of British Rail*)

Three views of Bradford Exchange – two of the station as it used to be and one as it never was.

Top: The fine roof, clock, vehicular access and parcels area feature in this 8th May, 1968 view looking towards the city end.

Centre: Before the bus/rail interchange was thought of, British Rail had its own plans to modernise Exchange station, providing a grander if more contempory entrance, complete with escalators, as shown by this architect's model completed in June, 1965.

Bottom: An ancient scene looking through the old wooden ticket barriers to platforms 7 and 8 on 6th January, 1959. Equally antique gas lights hang overhead while on the left is one of the roller departure indicators popularised by the North Eastern Region and, occupying one of the platforms, a rake of wooden suburban coaches. (*all by courtesy of British Rail*)

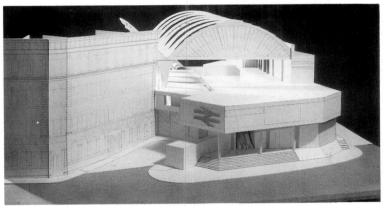

Under the magnificent arcading that covered Exchange station's 10 platforms.
Above: Although the Fairburn 2-6-4Ts predominated, Low Moor had a small number of the earlier variety designed by Sir William Stanier. Here, No.42616, displaced from working Chester–Birkenhead locals, finds itself at the head of through coaches to Kings Cross in summer, 1967.
Below: Jubilee No.45562 *Alberta* waits to be relieved of its coaches after arriving with the summer Saturday Poole–Bradford train on 30th July, 1966. Originally routed via Huddersfield, Sheffield and the Great Central main line, this train continued to run, via Huddersfield, Sheffield and Birmingham until 1987. The engine had just been transferred to Leeds Holbeck depot upon closure of Farnley Junction. (*both Barry Mounsey*)

The last of Thompson's 410 LNER Class B1 4-6-0s and one of the last steam-hauled trains from Exchange station. This powerful yet poignant view of No.61306 was taken on 30th September, 1967 as she waited to leave with the 22.00 parcels to Huddersfield. Earlier that day, 61306 had already worked the last steam Yorkshire Pullman. Following the end of steam the next day and the closure of Low Moor shed, she was moved to Carnforth depot, Lancashire, where she was prepared for a new life in preservation. (*Barry Mounsey*)

Top: Already minus nameplates, Wakefield B1 No.61013 *Topi* has just arrived with a parcels train from Normanton on 8th June, 1966 while one of Hammerton Street's Metro-Cammell DMUs forms a local service on the left. (*Brian Myland*)

Centre: Fowler 2-6-4T No.42411 awaits departure on 30th March, 1964 with the 09.27 Kings Cross portion which would join the main train from Leeds at Wakefield. This train included through carriages from Huddersfield and Halifax. (*Barry Mounsey*)

Bottom: Less usual if not unheard of power for an express passenger train. Stockport Edgeley 8F 2-8-0 No.48267 waits to take out the 09.07 to Poole on 3rd September, 1966. (*Michael Leahy*)

Top: Hughes-Fowler Crab 2-6-0s put in years of hard work over the L&Y line from Bradford and 42863, previously a Huddersfield engine, would have been no stranger. On 2nd August, 1961, when a Wakefield engine, it waits to leave platform 8 with an unidentified express. (*Peter Rose*)

Centre: Hammerton Street depot had an allocation of BR/Gardner 204hp 0-6-0 diesel shunters (latterly Class 03) which were regular Exchange/Interchange station pilots until the early 1980s. They also worked as far away as Halifax and Sowerby Bridge on goods and coal shunts. No.D2173 is pictured at Exchange station in the 1960s. (*Michael Leahy*)

Bottom: The diesels are taking over on 3rd June, 1965. Metro-Cammell and Calder Valley DMUs stand on the left as Deltic No.D9008 *The Green Howards* prepares to head for Kings Cross with the Yorkshire Pullman. (*Roy Wood*)

SHORT MEMORIES

Summer, 1960: Low Moor 2-6-4Ts regularly work the Halifax–St Pancras service to Sheffield Midland via Thornhill Jn and Barnsley.

August, 1960: Ardsley-based K3 2-6-0s are being used daily on Bradford Exchange to Blackpool services, including the 8.25am outward and the 7.33pm return.

Thousands of farewells will have been said at a big station like Bradford Exchange over the years but none as sad as these which marked the end of a great era.

Below: Bradford–Stockport services, by then one of the longest workings in the country for a tank engine, ended on 5th November, 1966. Here, the last train waits to leave Exchange with Fairburn 2-6-4T No.42116 in charge.

Right: It is Sunday 1st October, 1967 and the steam age is ending so far as Bradford is concerned. Fairburn tank No.42152 prepares to leave with 1E83, the 16.18 through coaches to Kings Cross, the last s t e a m - h a u l e d B r a d f o r d – L e e d s passenger train. (both Barry Mounsey)

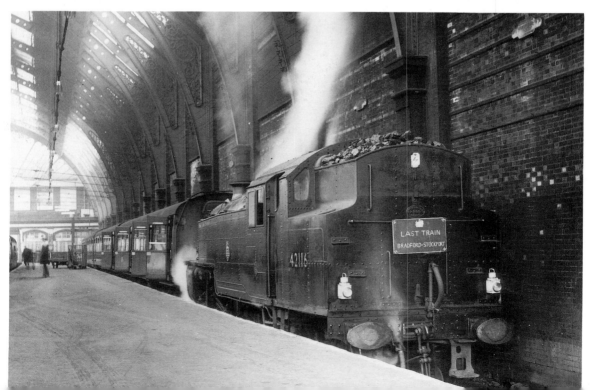

SHORT MEMORIES

October, 1960: Man-ningham Compound 41063 is withdrawn and sent to Doncaster works for scrap.

January 1962: Purpose-built 720 hp 3-car Calder Valley DMUs take over from steam on Liverpool–Bradford/Leeds trains. Instead of separate Bradford and Leeds portions combining and dividing at Low Moor, is a new Liverpool–Bradford–Leeds–Harrogate service.

27.5.63: A3 4-6-2 60038 *Firdaussi* arrives at Hammerton Street depot with two diesel shunters from Hull.

8.9.63: BR Class 6 4-6-2 72008 *Clan Macleod* works the morning Stourton–Bradford Valley pick-up goods before travelling light engine to Skipton shed.

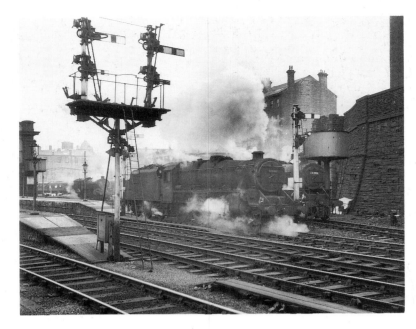

Above: Action on the east side of Exchange station on 6th August, 1966 as Black Five No.44946 storms out of platform 10 past Fairburn tank No.42116 and through a fine collection of traditional railway infrastructure. (*Michael Leahy*)

Below: Autumn, 1961 saw weekend trains between Leeds and Kings Cross diverted via Low Moor and Wakefield because of engineering work. As a result, the main trains ran to and from Bradford with the portions serving Leeds Central, bringing top link East Coast power to Exchange. On 17th September, A1 4-6-2 No. 60134 *Foxhunter* is ready for the off while A3 No. 60063 *Isinglass* has been relieved of its train and is waiting the 'peg' to leave the station. (*D. Butterfield*)

Above: The view from platform 10 to the carriage sidings on 8th June, 1966 with Wakefield Jubilee No.45739 *Ulster* in attendance. The Vicar Lane goods depot, shown in the front cover picture, was closed in April, 1958 and demolished around 1965. *(Brian Myland)*

Below: B1 4-6-0 No.61306 steam heats the stock for the Bradford portion of the Yorkshire Pullman on Saturday 30th September, 1967 before taking the last steam-hauled working of this train to Leeds. The locomotive looks in remarkably good condition to say it is working its last day at the end of steam when most engines were becoming rusty, leaking heaps, and reflects great credit on Low Moor staff and the enthusiasts who supported them. *(Barry Mounsey)*

Although the huge Bridge Street goods depot alongside Exchange station handled general freight, the warehouse pictured was for receiving and storing vast tonnages of wool.
Top: Scammel Scarab mechanical drays are loaded with bales of wool ready for delivery on 6th May, 1959. The goods offices are on the right, the town hall clock tower is just visible on the left, while in the centre of the picture is evidence that capstains were used for moving wagons around the depot. Just out of the picture on the left is the single-storey general goods shed. (*by courtesy of British Rail*)
Right: Another view from the yard looking towards the offices a couple of years later. Bridge Street closed on 22nd October, 1962. (*Michael Leahy*)

Robert Anderson began his railway career in late 1961 as a junior clerk in the office at Bridge Street wool warehouse.

"It was a very dark and dingy place with very tall stools and sloping desks, though it had progressed to electric lighting.

"I started work at 6am and by 6.30 the mill owners themselves, people like Kassapian's, were ringing up with the code numbers of bales of wool they wanted moving from one part of the warehouse to another that day.

"Another job I had was dealing with coal waybills which had nothing to do with Bradford. They were for movements of coal from places like Woolley Colliery, near Barnsley, to, say, Skipton. There must have been some sort of arrangement whereby waybills were sent to our depot for charging.

"Capstains were used for moving wagons around the yard and there were electric cranes for moving wool around the warehouse. Iron spiral staircases wrapped around the main support pillars provided access between floors.

"The last horse-drawn mill dray in Bradford used to come in each day from Robert Jowitt's for bales of wool. The horse was called Duke.

"I had only been at Bridge Street a few months when it closed and I moved to Valley which had altogether more modern surroundings. There wasn't so much wool there. I was on forwarding and late turn shipping.

"When on mornings I was at Valley and, if on the evening shift, I was at Trafalgar where I had to stamp every consignment note – even the smallest of packages had a consignment note.

"I usually managed to get out and see the three evening express freights waiting to depart with engines like Royal Scots and Jubilees displaced from the Midland main line. They stood in line alongside each other before backing onto their trains."

In the last years of steam, Bradford Exchange was a popular venue for enthusiasts wishing to observe the thunderous departures up the 1 in 50 gradient of its summer Saturday expresses to the East and West coasts.

Left: On 9th July, 1966 Black Five No.45395 of Wigan Springs Branch shed begins its ascent with the 08.20 to Bridlington.

Below: One of Holbeck's last Jubilees, No.45697 *Achilles*, steels itself for the assault to Bowling Junction with the 09.10 to Blackpool North on 10th June, 1967. Even at this late stage there is still plenty of steam around Bradford and Fairburn 2-6-4T No.42138 waits clearance to enter the station with the daily parcels from Normanton. Bridge Street goods depot is clear of wagons, having been closed for nearly five years. (*both Brian Myland*)

Top: B1 superpower as 61017 *Bushbuck* and 61189 *Sir William Gray* begin the slog up to Laisterdyke with the 08.02 to Skegness on Saturday 10th July, 1965. This portion travelled via the Wortley curve in Leeds to Wakefield where it joined the train from Leeds.

Bottom: On 20th May, 1965, Fowler 2-6-4T No.42317 was shunting the station sidings. (*both Brian Myland*)

Right: Victorian working conditions in Bradford Exchange signal box yet this picture was taken as recently as 23rd November, 1970. Only one box, Mill Lane, was required in 1993 to control the entire south side of Bradford. (*by courtesy of British Rail*)

Dramatic departures from Bradford Exchange:

Above: Getting away with three smartly turned out Mk1 coaches forming the Bradford portion of the southbound White Rose in 1962 is B1 No.61274. The present Interchange station was opened on this spot in 1973, though it retained the Exchange name until the complete Interchange incorporating the bus station was opened in 1977.

Left: A special train storms the bank with well-polished Jubilee No.45694 *Bellerophon* in charge on 6th August, 1963.

Below: Double-heading a heavy train to Bridlington on the same day were Black Five No.44694 and B1 No.61291. (*all Michael Leahy*)

Mill Lane Junction, where the L&Y line to Halifax and the GN line to Leeds part company, was probably the most photographed spot in Bradford during the last summer of steam. That was because of the simultaneous departures which ran neck and neck to the junction before going their separate ways.

Top: Black Five No.44693 and Fairburn tank No.42073 reach Mill Lane in classic style with Easter trains on 27th March, 1967. (*Michael Leahy*)

Centre: On 8th July, 1967 No.73141, one of the Caprotti valve gear BR Standard Class 5 4-6-0s allocated to Patricroft shed, Manchester, was heading the 08.20 to Bridlington. Stanier 2-6-4T No.42616 was banking at the rear. (*Brian Myland*)

Bottom: Also providing assistance up to Bowling Junction, this time on 31st May, 1966 was Ivatt Class 4 2-6-0 No.43137 at the rear of Whit Tuesday special No.1X54. The Leeds line curves away to the left while St Dunstan's carriage sidings are in the centre. (*Brian Myland*)

Top: Photographers capture the moment when Stanier 2-6-4T No.42616 brings up the rear of the 08.20 to Bridlington via Halifax on 8th July, 1967. Behind the engine are Springmill Street coal drops which were still there, disused since 1983, at the time of publication.

Centre: Making a fine sight with Whit Tuesday excursion 1X54 on 31st May, 1966 is well kept Black Five No.45449. Ivatt 2-6-0 No.43137 is banking at the rear.

Bottom: Descending the bank this time, Wakefield B1 No.61024 *Addax* brings the Normanton vans over Mill Lane Junction on 2nd March, 1966. This picture was taken from beneath Mill Lane signal box with St Dunstan's box just 150 yards away in the background. (*all Brian Myland*)

Passenger trains may, when necessary, be assisted out of Bradford Exchange by a locomotive in the rear. The driver of the train must be informed that it will be assisted to start by a locomotive in the rear … The assisting locomotive must not be attached to the train …
Eastern Region Northern Area Sectional Appendix, 1968.

Springmill Street, situated on the west side of Mill Lane Junction was the last goods yard on the south side of Bradford. Coal, its predominent traffic ceased in November, 1983 and the yard closed completely with effect from 7th July, 1984, the site now a go-kart track.

The trip working which used one of Hammerton Street's Class 08 350hp diesels to collect and deliver coal wagons is pictured (top) entering the yard in August, 1980 while the Hammerton Street travelling shunter and Springmill Street's shunter (centre) present a timeless scene. (both Malcolm Roughley)

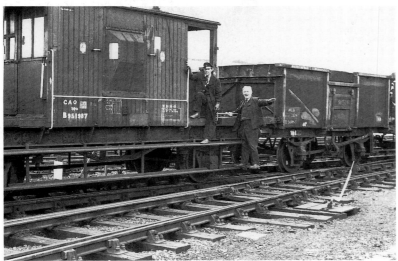

Bottom: Ripley Street was the spot where the L&Y line to Halifax crossed over the GN's Queensbury line. On 16th July, 1966 B1 No.61115 and three empty coaches from Exchange station turn on the St Dunstan's triangle. The engine propelled its train from Exchange to St Dunstan's East on the Leeds line. It is now drawing forward to St Dunstan's South before going under the bridge to cross over and reverse back through the former St Dunstan's station to Exchange. (Brian Myland)

Vintage Lanky at Ripley Street.
Above: On 2nd July, 1936, Mirfield-based Aspinall 2-4-2T, LMS No.10841 with round-topped firebox and extended coal bunker, ascends the bank past Coal Shutes signal box with a local train. This engine was scrapped before 1945 and the signal box demolished between 1964 and 1965. (*G.H.Butland*)
Below: With the turnouts to Springmill Street depot on the left, Aspinall 3F 0-6-0 No.52413, one of the batch rebuilt from 1911 with Belpaire fireboxes and extended smokeboxes, heads a goods south from Bradford in the mid-1950s. (*Peter Sunderland*)

More vintage views at Ripley Street.
Top: No.1199, one of four LMS Compound 4-4-0s allocated to Low Moor from 1930 to 1946, heads a stopping train up the bank on 22nd July, 1936.
Centre: Bowling shed had 14 N1 0-6-2Ts at nationalisation which saw plenty of use on the Queensbury lines to Keighley and Halifax. No.69478 heads for Queensbury underneath the L&Y line on 16th October, 1950.
Bottom: Low Moor Black Five No.5207 heads the time-honoured Bradford to Bournemouth express(which ceased running 50 years later) on 5th May, 1937. The first coach is a Southern Railway vehicle and the rest LNER, emphasising this train's historic link with the Great Central Railway which it will reach via Huddersfield and Penistone. (all G.H.Butland)

Top: With no trains to obscure the view on 1st July, 1964, the layout around St Dunstan's can be clearly seen. From left are: Springmill Street coal yard, the L&Y loop and main lines, Coal Shutes signal box, St Dunstan's carriage sidings and, on the St Dunstan's South-West curve, the Queensbury line platforms which closed along with the rest of the station on 15th September, 1952.

Centre: The next railway location south of Ripley Street was Bowling Junction where 8F 2-8-0 No.48721 is seen taking the avoiding line to Laisterdyke on 26th May, 1965. Also pictured are the signal box, the site of the station and the entrance to Bowling Tunnel. The junction was removed following rerouting via Leeds in 1985 of the avoiding line's last regular train, a trip serving J. McIntyre's scrap yard at Laisterdyke, which until then had travelled from Healey Mills via Halifax. (both Brian Myland)

Bottom: Bowling Junction station, closed on 3rd December, 1951, seen looking towards the junction shortly before closure. (by courtesy of the Bradford Telegraph and Argus)

50

Far from being a backwater, the Laisterdyke–Bowling Junction line carried main line traffic, passenger and goods, which did not need to call and therefore reverse at Bradford Exchange.

Equipped with absolute block signalling and intermediate signal boxes at Bowling and Hall Lane, and with a 50 mph maximum speed, it formed a short cut between Leeds and Halifax which would be very useful today.

The line was closed, however, to passenger trains in 1969 and to goods in September, 1985, although by then it was no longer a through route but terminated alongside McIntyre's scrap yard. Closure was enabled by the reinstatement of connections onto the main line at Laisterdyke but the scrap traffic ended soon after. Most of the line was lifted in 1987 though the post-September, 1985 layout at the Laisterdyke end survived, disused, in 1993.

Top and Bottom: Wakefield WD 2-8-0 No.90300 passes Hall Lane signal box and level crossing with what is probably a Healey Mills to Laisterdyke goods on 2nd June, 1965. (*Brian Myland*)

SHORT MEMORIES

September, 1963: New Clayton Type 1 diesel No.D8501, based at Ardsley for trials, works mineral trips to City Road via Bramley and returns via Tingley. The loco also works trips to Shipley via Idle, returning from Quarry Gap via Batley.

26.9.63: D8501 fails at Heckmondwyke while trying to work 26 loaded coal wagons from Healey Mills to Ardsley via Low Moor, Bowling and Laisterdyke.

September 1963: Stanier 8P 4-6-2 No.46247 *City of Liverpool* is hauled dead through Shipley heading for Birmingham.

26.9.63: Stanier 8P 4-6-2 No.46238 *City of Carlisle* arrives light at Shipley from the Skipton direction and returns after turning on the triangle.

Top: Just three quarters of a mile from Laisterdyke on the avoiding line were a station and signal box at Bowling. The station closed as long ago as 1st February, 1895 but was still intact when this westbound empty Metro-Cammell DMU was passing through on 2nd June, 1965. (*Brian Myland*) The accompanying goods yard lasted until 4th May, 1964 and a private siding for a while longer.

Below: The GN line from Bradford was dogged by steep gradients, starting with the 1 in 50 from almost a standing start at Exchange station to St Dunstan's and steepening to 1 in 49 before reaching the summit at Laisterdyke. Departures from Bradford were made even more difficult by the sharp curve through St Dunstan's and even the 1990s Sprinter trains find the climb taxing.

Against a backdrop of mill chimneys, one of the Gresley N2 0-6-2Ts allocated to Bradford shed for a time, No.4736, tackles the grade through a well-kept St Dunstan's station on 15th September, 1938. (*G.H.Butland*) The loco was renumbered 9515 in 1946 by which time it had returned to the Kings Cross suburban area.

When, owing to engine failure or any other cause, a train comes to a stand and is unable to proceed on a line in the vicinity of St Dunstan's which is track circuited, it must not be moved in the reverse direction until the signalman's permission has been obtained. Locomotives requiring to pass through the crossover road from the Up to the Down line at St Dunstan's East, and from the Down to the Up line at St Dunstan's West, must be brought to a stand as near as possible to the disc signal so that the locomotives may stand on the treadle bars ahead of the crossover road points. *Eastern Region Northern Area Sectional Appendix, 1968.*

Top: Four of Hammerton Street's 350hp Class 08 shunters occupied the repair shop on this day in August, 1980. The shop was equipped with an overhead crane, and a drop pit which was essential for removing the big Rolls Royce 180hp engines from the Calder Valley DMUs allocated there from 1961 onwards. *(Malcolm Roughley)*

Centre: Inside the maintenance shed on 6th May, 1984 with Metro-Cammell DMU 51433/51499 and Calder Valley car 51830 on view.

Bottom: On the same day, the running shed, which had been roofless since steam days, contained a good selection of Calder Valley units with 51842/59709/51813 present. *(both Alan Whitaker)*

SHORT MEMORIES

7.9.64: Local passenger trains between Wakefield, Dewsbury and Bradford Exchange are withdrawn.

15.10.64: A1 Pacific No.60154 *Bon Accord* heads a Hunslet–Carlisle freight through Shipley.

26.10.64: Jubilee No.45742 *Connaught* takes the 14.00 to Sheffield out of Forster Square.

28.10.64: Clan No.72005 *Clan Macgregor* heads the 21.30 Forster Square– St Pancras as far as Leeds after earlier working a stopping train from Carlisle.

14.6.65: Passenger services between Bradford Exchange and Huddersfield via Heckmondwyke, Mirfield and Halifax, are withdrawn. Low Moor is among stations closed. Bradford–Stockport and Halifax–Kings Cross through services are not affected.

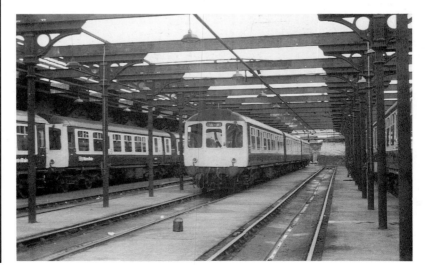

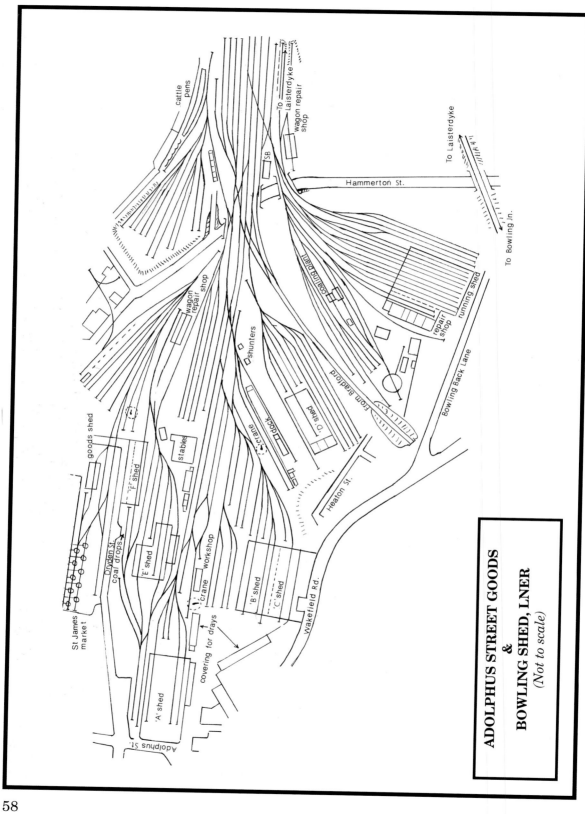

ADOLPHUS STREET GOODS
&
BOWLING SHED, LNER
(Not to scale)

The GNR's first station in Bradford was Adolphus Street, opened in 1854. It was relegated to a goods depot in 1867 when passenger trains were transferred over the newly-opened Hammerton Street-Mill Lane line to the L&Y's Drake Street station which was enlarged and renamed Exchange.

The Adolphus Street station, with its arched roof rising 50ft above the platforms, was one of several warehouses occupying a vast goods yard site. It became known as 'A' shed, but there were also the combined 'B' and 'C' sheds alongside Wakefield Road, which formed a four-storey wool warehouse, 'D' shed, a single-road goods depot off Heaton Street which had a small adjoining yard latterly used by John Hornby scrap dealers, the two-road 'E' shed (handling fruit), and the single-road 'F' shed in Dryden Street which was used as a banana and potato warehouse. The whole complex closed on 1st May, 1972 and 21 years later the site was occupied by modern warehouses.

Top: The original station frontage on 12th February, 1967. The inscription in the stonework reads 'Great Northern Railway Goods and Coal Department'. (*D. Butterfield*)

Centre and Bottom: Inside and outside the Adolphus Street wool warehouse (B and C sheds) on 6th May, 1959. (*both by courtesy of Brtitish Rail*)

Misfortune befell Adolphus Street on at least two occasions within six years.

Top and centre: On the morning of 11th November, 1964 Ivatt Class 4 2-6-0 No.43072 ran out of control down the side of the old GNR station, crashing through a wall and finishing up in the street below. The crew jumped clear and no-one was injured but the engine was terminally damaged and had to be cut up on the spot by a local scrap merchant. (*both Michael Leahy*)

Bottom: A hardly more appropriate date for the destruction by fire of the banana warehouse on Dryden Street was 5th November, 1958. (*by courtesy of British Rail*)

SHORT MEMORIES

14.6.65: With the summer timetable The Cornishman to Penzance starts running from Bradford instead of starting at Sheffield.

14.6.65: The Devonian to Paignton is speeded up by 22 minutes and extended to Plymouth and Kingswear.

Summer, 1965: Jubilee No.45643 *Rodney* (55C) is a regular performer on the Saturdays Only Bradford Exchange to Bournemouth as far as Sheffield. The train is composed of SR green coaches on alternate weekends.

12.9.65: From this date Sunday Bradford–Kings Cross services start running to and from Forster Square via Leeds City and Wakefield Kirkgate for the winter timetable, with journey times increased by up to 11 minutes.

Seaside specials climbing up to Laisterdyke on 8th August, 1964.
Above: B1 4-6-0 No.61014 *Oribi* between Hammerton Street and Laisterdyke with the 07.48 Bradford to Skegness, which took the Dudley Hill line to Dewsbury Central and Wakefield Westgate where it combined with a similar portion from Leeds Central. The avoiding line from Bowling Junction to Laisterdyke West is to the left of the train.
Below: Fairburn 2-6-4T No.42141 approaches Laisterdyke West Junction with the 08.52 Bradford to Cleethorpes, another train booked to run via Dewsbury. (*both Brian Myland*)

In summer 1946 the LNER station at Laisterdyke was served by 20 trains a day to Leeds Central via Pudsey, 10 via Stanningley, 13 to Wakefield Westgate and Kirkgate via Dudley Hill, Batley and Dewsbury Central, and 9 to Ardsley via Dudley Hill and Morley Top. Three of the Leeds via Stanningley trains were operated by the LMS and came either from Low Moor or Halifax via the avoiding line from Bowling Junction, though none of those in the opposite direction called at Laisterdyke.

Passing through (above) with an eastbound trip working on 19th July, 1961 was Low Moor J50 0-6-0T No.68923 and (right) going away towards Laisterdyke East Junction. The still extant Leeds line goes straight on and the Dudley Hill line to the right. (*both Peter Rose*)

Bottom: The Laisterdyke area in the early 1960s (*Not to scale*).

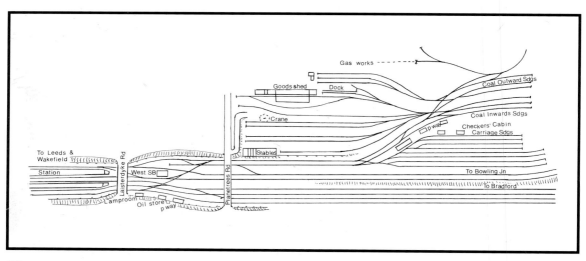

62

GAS BOARD'S SIDINGS. BIRKSHALL. A single-lever ground frame is provided adjacent to the connection leading from the Arrival line at Planetrees to the Gas Board's Outward sidings and the Empties bank, to control two signals, one situated at the outlet from the Empties bank and the other at the outlet from the goods yard sidings, which are provided to stop shunting movements between the goods yard and the Empties bank. These signals stand normally off with the lever over.

Locomotives and vehicles proceeding over the Arrival line to the Empties bank must be brought to a stand at the ground frame, and the guard or shunter in charge must satisfy himself that no conflicting movement is being made or is about to be made by a Gas Board locomotive ... and that the hand-worked double slip connections leading from the Gas Board's Outward sidings are so set as to prevent any movement to or from the Arrival line. The ground frame lever must then be replaced in the frame, which will bolt lock the points concerned and place both signals to danger.

Before any subsequent movement is made between the Empties bank and the goods yard sidings, the guard or shunter in charge must pull over the lever in the ground frame, and observe that the signals have responded ... *Eastern Region Northern Area Sectional Appendix, 1968.*

The above view from the west end of Laisterdyke station with two pairs of Class 04 diesel shunters undertaking trip duties on 8th April, 1968, belies what was happening just behind the buildings on the overbridge. The four-platform station, closed on 4th July, 1966, was being brutally raized as seen below. (*both Brian Myland*)

Bottom: Planetrees goods yard, Laisterdyke, was well filled with wagons of coal bound for the neighbouring Birkshall gas works when photographed by the Bradford Telegraph & Argus on 15th August, 1961. It officially closed on 11th September but continued to provide access to the gas works for a few more years. The site was since occupied by J. McIntyre's who regularly sent out scrap by rail until 1986. The goods shed was still standing in 1993.

GREAT NORTHERN TO THE EAST

Until the mass closures of the 1960s, there were four exits from Bradford to the east, all originating with the GNR. These were to Leeds via Stanningley and Pudsey, to Shipley, and to Wakefield via Dudley Hill – a line which in turn sent off another important route to Wakefield via Dewsbury.

The focal point for all these lines was Laisterdyke where a conglomeration of junctions made up a complex and busy layout. Here too was Quarry Gap yard, a collection and distribution point for goods traffic to and from GNR depots in the Bradford area.

Top: The GNR signal box at Laisterdyke East Junction, viewed from a passing train on 20th September, 1969. Access to Quarry Gap yard is under the bridge in the centre background. (*M.A. King*)

Centre: This view just east of the signal box on 10th May, 1965 shows WD 2-8-0 90678 leaving Quarry Gap in the Bradford direction. The overbridge through which it has passed carries Dick Lane and has since been filled in.

Bottom: Looking west from Dick Lane over the entrance to Quarry Gap yard and towards Laisterdyke East box with Ivatt 2-6-0 No.43096 on 12th May, 1965. (*Both Brian Myland*)

Quarry Gap on 10th May, 1961.

Top: Looking East from Dick Lane bridge with a 204hp diesel shunter marshalling wagons and B1 4-6-0 No.61023 *Hirola* on a train. The Stanningley line to Leeds – the only GN route from Bradford left in 1993 – is in a cutting behind the brick hut.

Centre: From the same bridge with the Stanningley line on the left. Like many former railway sites, this view is now filled with modern warehouses and light industrial units.

Bottom: Looking west towards Laisterdyke with B1 No.61259 manouvring wagons. The recently singled track coming from the left is from Cutler's Junction on the Dudley Hill line which along with the Shipley branch (right of the loco) formed a triangle. Rising to the left is Quarry Gap Siding, a small goods yard which by 1968 was classed as a private siding for W & J Whitehead's textile mill, visible on the horizon. (*all Brian Myland*)

Bottom: No.61259 extends past Quarry Gap signal box and onto the Shipley branch during shunting movements at the east end of the yard. Immediately behind the engine is the intersection bridge over the Leeds line, and on the horizon the English Electric company's Dick Lane foundry, Thornbury, which was served by a private siding where a 1949-built Ruston and Hornsby diesel was kept for shunting until the mid-1970s.

Top: The Shipley branch was intended as a suburban passenger link between Bradford's north and south rail systems and had well-appointed stations built in a distinctive style, but it also carried a fair amount of freight. The passenger service ceased as early as 2nd February, 1931 but the stations, like Eccleshill, remained mostly intact.

Centre: The Laisterdyke–Idle section closed completely on 2nd November, 1964 (save for the connection to English Electric's foundry) and Ivatt Class 4 2-6-0 No.43051 was making one of the last trips to Eccleshill goods yard when photographed with just two coal wagons on 17th October. *(all Brian Myland)*

Idle on 17th October, 1964.

Top: The disused station looking south towards the goods yard, Eccleshill and Laisterdyke.

Centre: Looking north towards Shipley. For a number of years the Bradford Railway Circle had a clubroom in the station buildings.

Bottom: Idle goods yard survived, served by a 2 mile 645 yard single track from Shipley, worked usually by a Holbeck Class 25 diesel, until it too succumbed on 7th October, 1968. By then the Idle branch was worked under 'One Engine in Steam' regulations (no signalling and only one train allowed on the branch at a time) with a 25 mph speed limit. Here, Ivatt Class 4 No.43051 prepares to take its two coal wagons down to Eccleshill. (all Brian Myland)

Above: On the tops near Woodhall, between Shipley and Idle. In very early BR days an N1 0-6-2T and a B1 4-6-0 climb steadily with a special southbound passenger train composed of LNER wooden-bodied stock. (*H.L.Overend/National Railway Museum*)

Below: Class J39 0-6-0 No.64903 hauls a well-loaded goods up the 1 in 248 from Shipley Windhill in the mid-1950s. The Midland Leeds–Skipton line is down below. (*Peter Sunderland*)

Top: Approaching Shipley, the Idle branch split into two single lines, one to the Midland line at Leeds Junction and the other, 394 yards long and with a 5 mph speed limit, to Windhill goods yard. On 7th September, 1964, Black Five No.44896 leaves the goods yard and returns to Laisterdyke after bringing in a trip working. (*Brian Myland*)

Centre: J6 0-6-0 No.64271 prepares for the return to Laisterdyke after shunting its pick-up goods at Windhill yard on 8th October, 1949. An extra brake van has been added behind the engine for members of the Bradford Railway Circle. Windhill goods yard closed on 7th October, 1968. (*G.H.Butland*)

Bottom: Shipley & Windhill passenger station, closed on 2nd February, 1931, was visited in 1953 by this Stephenson Locomotive Society railtour hauled by N1 0-6-2T No.69430. Forty years later the station was still standing, used by second hand car and furniture dealers. On the right is Leeds Junction signal box. (*Peter Sunderland*)

Between Laisterdyke East and Cutler's Junction.

Top: Two eras of Bradford motive power meet on 8th August, 1964 as B1 No.61189 *Sir William Gray* gets the 08.27 Bradford Exchange to Yarmouth on its way to Wakefield where it will be joined by the 08.48 from Leeds. Approaching Laisterdyke East in the other direction is a Calder Valley DMU forming the 08.03 from Wakefield via Dewsbury.

Bottom: WD 2-8-0 90281 rounds the curve towards Cutler's Junction with a goods for Ardsley on 14th June, 1965. The spur to Quarry Gap goes off to the right while in the centre is another part of Quarry Gap Siding.

Centre: Passing the closed Cutler's Junction signal box on a different occasion in 1965, 90281 heads an engineers train towards Dudley Hill. Curving away left is the Pudsey loop which is in the course of abandonment. By 1993 the whole cutting had long been filled in and made into a level pasture. (*all Brian Myland*)

Top: Dudley Hill station, pictured with its large goods yard on 30th June, 1964, closed on 7th April, 1952 but the line through it from Laisterdyke to Ardsley, where it joined the Leeds–Doncaster line, continued in use until 1966. After closure as a through route, a one and a half-mile double track was retained from Laisterdyke East to Dudley Hill goods yard (reduced to a public delivery siding in 1965) until 1981 to serve steel stockholders Henry Barrett and Sons Ltd and the scrap yard of Arnott, Young and Co. With a maximum speed of 20 mph, the surviving lines were worked under 'One Engine in Steam' regulations. During the 1970s, the Royal Train was occasionally stabled overnight on the branch. (*Brian Myland*)

Below: Awaiting scrapping by Arnott, Young and Co in the goods yard at a point just left of the station buildings on 4th March, 1976 was ex-BR Yorkshire Engine Co 0-4-0 diesel shunter No.02001. (*Keith Preston*)

Guards working Down freight trains, both ordinary and special, for the City Road direction must, if necessary, stop at Dudley Hill on weekdays only to reduce their loads. Wagons that have to be detached at Dudley Hill must be placed next to the locomotive. On Sundays, trains must be reduced at Laisterdyke. *Eastern Region Northern Area Sectional Appendix, 1968.*

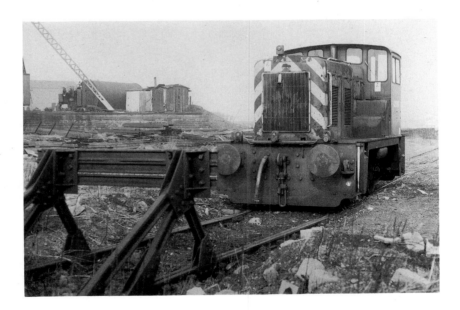

A loud gong is provided in the tunnel at the Birkenshaw end of Dudley Hill station to control setting back movements on the Up main line towards Nos.1 and 2 sidings via No.27 points. This gong is operated by a plunger located adjacent to No.28 disc signal, and when it is necessary for a driver who has drawn forward into the tunnel on the Up main to set back into 1 and 2 sidings under the instructions of the guard, the latter must control the movements ... by operating the bell plunger provided. *Eastern Region Northern Area Sectional Appendix, 1968.*

Top: Birkenshaw and Tong closed to passengers on 5th October, 1953 and the goods yard on 7th September, 1964. Only the bare platforms survived by the time Fairburn tank No.42116 was caught approaching the typically GN signal box with the 10.28 Bradford–Kings Cross on 30th October, 1966. Bradford portions of Kings Cross trains were diverted back onto this line on Sundays during that month because of engineering work.

Centre: Drighlington and Adwalton station survived until 1st January, 1962, after which it was no longer served by Wakefield to Bradford via Dewsbury trains like this one seen passing through on 4th July, 1964 when two years of disuse was taking its toll. (*both Brian Myland*)

Bottom: No.42116 again makes good progress through Drighlington on 2nd October, 1966 with the diverted 13.20 from Kings Cross. (*Peter Sunderland*)

The Cutler's Junction–Bramley via Pudsey line closed to passengers on 15th June, 1964 and to goods three weeks later. Back in 1946 it carried a busy commuter service with 20 stopping trains each way a day between Bradford and Leeds – more than the surviving route through Stanningley – but by 1961 they had already been halved.

On 13th February, 1965 it presented a depressing scene with demolition turning it into yet another Beeching casualty.

Top: The once sizeable Pudsey Greenside station and goods yard, looking towards Leeds, is almost trackless and about to be wiped out.

Centre: The demolition men had yet to butcher the smaller Pudsey Lowtown, seen looking towards Leeds, but had got to work on the Bradford side of the station (bottom) and the goods yard on the right. (all Brian Myland)

Just about the only stretch of open countryside left to be seen from a train in the Bradford area is on the Leeds via Stanningley line between Laisterdyke and Duckett's Crossing – a user-operated gated level crossing.

Top: B1 4-6-0 No.61161 may be grimy but it makes a delightful picture in its sylvan setting while approaching Duckett's Crossing in July, 1963 with the Bradford portion of the Yorkshire Pullman. (*Michael Leahy*)

Below: Of special interest at Duckett's Crossing was this automatic-return GNR somersault signal, seen returning itself to danger after the passage of a Bradford to Leeds Metro-Cammell DMU on 19th July, 1961. (*Peter Rose*)

LEEDS (WORTLEY WEST JN.) – BRADFORD EXCHANGE: 1968

Max speed on main lines 60mph
Max speed on goods lines....................................40mph

Signalling:

Absolute Block (Track Circuit Block between Bramley and Laisterdyke East).

Additional lines:

Wortley West-Bramley station: Up & Down Goods.
Armley Moor: Down refuge siding with standage for 34 wagons, engine and brake van.
Bramley Stn: Two Down refuge sidings with standage for 34 wagons, engine and brake van, and 33 wagons, engine and brake van. Up refuge siding with standage for 37 wagons, engine and brake van.
Laisterdyke East-West: Up and Down Slow.
Laisterdyke West-Hammerton Street: Down Goods.
Hammerton Street: Up refuge siding with standage for 150 wagons, engine and brake van.
Mill Lane Jn.– Bradford Exchange: Up and Down West.

Signal boxes:
(including distances between them)

Wortley West (0 miles 1083 yds from Holbeck West Jn.)
Armley Moor (0 miles 1287 yds)
Bramley (1 mile 1721 yds)
Laisterdyke East (3 miles 604 yds)
Laisterdyke West (0 miles 467 yds)
Hammerton Street (0 miles 1160 yds)
St Dunstan's (0 miles 1155 yds)
Mill Lane (0 miles 159 yds)
Exchange (0 miles 595 yds)

Gradients:

1 in 50 rising (Wortley West-Bramley)
1 in 147/100/98 rising (Bramley-Laisterdyke East)
1 in 100/58 falling (Laisterdyke East-West)
1 in 49 falling (Laisterdyke West-St Dunstan's)
1 in 50 falling (St Dunstan's-Exchange)

The new order is on its way. Black Five No.44826 pauses at New Pudsey station (opened 6th March, 1967) with the Bradford portion of the 09.25 from Kings Cross on 29th April, 1967. Under construction is the concrete 'cut and cover' tunnel to carry the Stanningley by-pass. One of the new concept of park and ride stations designed to meet the growth of car ownership, New Pudsey was meant to be used by passengers driving there from a wide catchment area. (*Brian Myland*)

Top: Replaced by New Pudsey, just a short distance to the west, Stanningley station closed on 31st December, 1967. With closure still 18 months away and the station looking neat and tidy, Fairburn 2-6-4T No.42055 hurries the 10.00 Bradford–Leeds portion of the Yorkshire Pullman past the unusually transverse signal box on 2nd July, 1966.

Centre: Stanningley still looked well kept on the day before closure as a railwayman in contemporary uniform watched the arrival of the 13.05 Bradford–Leeds DMU.

Bottom: To see a London-bound Pullman train in full flight behind steam as late as summer, 1967 may seem unlikely but it happened every day on this line. On 21st August, Black Five No.44694 was in charge of the Yorkshire Pullman from Bradford, watched by the crew of B1 No.61337 on local goods duty. Moments later 61337 derailed its front bogie on points in Stanningley goods yard. *(all Brian Myland)*

SHORT MEMORIES

Autumn, 1965: BR Clan Pacifics based at Carlisle take up regular work on the 15.40 Forster Square–Carlisle stopping train.

10.6.66: Three special trains from Bradford Exchange to Blackpool for staff of Grattan's catalogue warehouse are all double-headed. Black Fives 45368 & 44946 are on train 1X40, 44694 & Jubilee No.45565 *Victoria* are on 1X41, and 44951 & 45694 *Bellerophon* are on 1X42.

Above: With the end of steam in the area just a month away, B1 No.61306 leaves Stanningley yard and passes Stanningley East signal box with the morning coal trip to Armley Moor on 25th August, 1967. Stanningley goods yard remained in operation until 11th October, 1979. (*Brian Myland*)

Below: The layout at Stanningley in 1956 (*not to scale*).

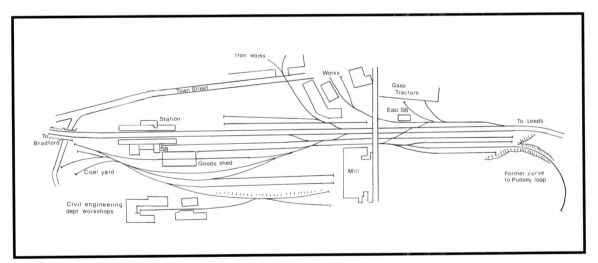

Right: George Cohen engineers had a works yard at Stanningley which was shunted by two industrial saddle tanks, including this 0-4-0 built in 1913 by Kitson of Leeds. (*John Holroyd*)

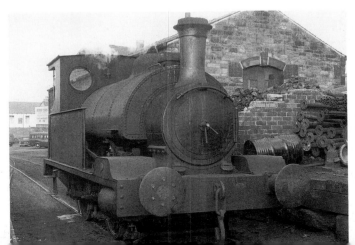

Top: Bramley station looking towards Bradford on 14th February, 1965 with the Pudsey loop curving away left beyond the signal box. The station closed on 4th July, 1966 and only the two main tracks ultimately survived, but a timber halt was opened on roughley the same site by West Yorkshire PTE in 1983.

Last day at Armley Moor station as two steam-hauled expresses speed through on 2nd July, 1966: Fairburn tank 42073 (bottom) heads for Bradford with the 07.45 from Kings Cross, while (centre) 42177 races through with the Bradford portion of the 09.18 from Cleethorpes. (all Brian Myland)

Derek Amos retired in 1993 after 51 years of railway service during which he estimates that he worked 40 different signal boxes in the Bradford area. He spent most of his working life on the south side, starting work with the LNER in 1942 as a weighbridge lad at Dudley Hill.

"The traffic we handled at Dudley Hill was nearly all coal for merchants who, with it being wartime, piled up big stocks in case of shortages. We also had steel coming in for Henry Barrett's, the structural engineers, some farm traffic and quite a lot of wool. The wool was kept in a two-storey warehouse with a crane powered by a gas engine upstairs, but sometimes there was so much that it had to be stacked outside and sheeted over."

After moving on to become a telegraph lad at Laisterdyke East, Mr. Amos got his first signalman's job at Great Horton in 1948.

"The box there had a rocker frame, you could stand on it and it threw the lever towards you – the locking fitters said it was the only one in this district.

"We regarded Great Horton as not terribly busy. It was a Class 4 post dealing with around four passenger trains an hour and seven or eight goods trains a shift.

"It really got busy before the Bradford holiday weeks when coaching stock for excursion trains was stabled in the goods yard.

"I went on to Drighlington where we had seven push and pull trains a day to and from Ardsley for the miners. The goods yard had a Ministry of Food buffer depot which was full of sugar and lard during the war.

"From there I went to Cutler's Junction and then to Broad Lane which was a box situated between the Up and Down mains. There was an Up goods loop which was all we were there for.

"We also had the curve coming in from Tyersal Junction on the Pudsey loop which was only used as required. When they switched it in, it caused so many block failures that it wasn't worth the trouble and they decided to pack it in altogether.

"On the main lines we got a lot of empty wagons coming up the 1 in 55 from Laisterdyke. usually the trains had a banker but when there wasn't one they were split into two portions which the engine took separately to Dudley Hill where they were combined again.

"Some of the seaside excursions to places like Skegness were double-headed to Birkenshaw, the pilot coming off there and going back to Bradford to be the train engine for the next one up. When a banker was used it went as far as Dudley Hill.

"Between February and June, we used to have a train which started at Ardsley and spent all day going round by Drighlington, Pudsey and Bramley collecting rhubarb from local growers."

Following spells at boxes on the Queensbury line to Halifax, Mr Amos then went to Low Moor No.4 on the L&Y system.

"It was only a small box situated near the south end of Bowling Tunnel but you got everything that came off the loco. You were on the go all the time, day and night. When you had a pilot wanting to go from the Down to the Up sidings with four on, it could take 20 minutes to get him across, especially if there was a train from Liverpool in the station.

"When Hammerton Street went diesel it got very busy at Low Moor and it was like a game of roulette with engines trying to get off the shed.

"There were three lots of carriage sidings, one lot in the triangle, some behind the loco depot and more in front. Sometimes there were up to 170 coaches stabled there for weekend holiday trains. Friday night we would be waiting for stock coming in from the Southern Region to work trains to the south coast the next day.

"Low Moor mainly dealt with passenger traffic but there was some goods. Notable among express freights was the Aintree which was broken up and combined there. It was a very important train and had to leave on time.

"Bowling Tunnel used to tie us up. The majority of freights needed 14 minutes to get through which took some finding. This was because they had to go inside at Bowling Junction for the brakes to be pinned down for the steep gradient down the other side. Two or three ran away because the brakes hadn't been pinned down properly."

Mr Amos then became a relief signalman working at boxes all over the GN and L&Y lines in the area. One of them was Mill Lane.

"Mill Lane was very busy. It was very hard work with about 70 levers to operate and you had a lad to help.

"Towards the end of the 1960s, I was made redundant and found a job at Hall Lane on the Bowling–Laisterdyke line. It was very quiet, worked only day shifts and saw just seven trains a day carrying mainly coal and scrap between Healey Mills and Laisterdyke.

"In the early 1970s I had to move to Forster Square box where there was at that time a lot of parcels traffic to deal with. Seven trains left every night between 19.30 and 22.00 for places like Bristol, Birmingham, Manchester and York. After those you had a quiet hour then they would start forming trains up for the next day. At about 02.00 incoming parcels trains started rolling in and the shunters would be drawing them out to make them up into trains for later on. Most platforms were full of parcels trains being loaded during the day, sometimes with two trains in the same platform. When it came to Christmas you'd have to draw them out into the sidings so you could put some more in.

"At its peak, Forster Square had 70 parcels porters working three shifts then, suddenly, it all stopped, just like that when the railway lost the contract to the Post Office."

The GNR route going north west from Bradford led to a system which has fascinated railway students for generations. It led through the hills to Queensbury where there was a triangular station. Continuing north west, the line went on to Keighley while turning left at Queensbury sent trains south to Halifax. Passenger services were withdrawn on 23rd May, 1955 but goods traffic, mainly coal and timber continued as far as Thornton until 1965 when the line was cut back to serve only a coal depot at Horton Park and the branch to City Road. These remained in use until 28th August, 1972 after which they too were abandoned.

Top: Manchester Road was one of the first suburban stations in Bradford to be lost, closing as a wartime measure on 31st December, 1915 and never reopening. Half a century later, the platforms had gone but the station buildings on the overbridge remained in private use. This 13th May, 1965 view looking towards Queensbury was taken from the site of the goods yard, itself closed on 6th May, 1963.

Right: On 2nd June, 1965, B1 No.61386 worked the 07.05 goods from City Road to Laisterdyke and is seen approaching the GNR somersault signal protecting the junction with the Queensbury line at Horton Park. (*both Brian Myland*)

GREAT NORTHERN TO THE WEST

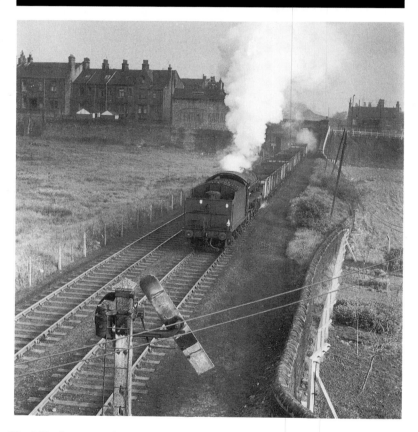

In summer, 1946 trains left Bradford Exchange at 5.55am, 11.5am, 12.10pm, 1.30pm, 3.55pm, 5.15pm, 5.45pm, 7.45pm and 10.27pm on weekdays for Keighley, calling at St Dunstan's, Horton Park, Great Horton, Clayton, Queensbury, Thornton, Denholme, Wilsden, Cullingworth and Ingrow, taking between 35 and 50 minutes end to end.

They left for Halifax (Old) at 5.40am, 6.30am, 7.15am, 7.54am, 8.57am, 10.8am, 10.44am, 12.50pm, 1.55pm, 3.30pm, 4.39pm, 6.0pm, 6.43pm, 9.15pm and 11pm, calling at St Dunstan's, Horton Park, Great Horton, Clayton, Queensbury, Holmfield, Ovenden and North Bridge. Not all trains called at St Dunstan's, Horton Park or Ovenden, while the 11pm from Bradford was non-stop taking 22 minutes. The average end to end journey time was 35 minutes compared with about 20 minutes over the L&Y line. There were also 12 trains each way between Halifax and Keighley and all interconnected at Queensbury.

The double track branch to City Road goods ran for 1 mile 1140 yards and included a 1 in 50/88 climb from Horton Junction. In the late 1960s it was operated according to special local instructions with a 10 mph speed limit although the section from St Dunstan's to Horton Park was still fully signalled, worked under absolute block from Horton Junction signal box.
Top: B1 No.61014 *Oribi* traverses Horton Junction on 10th June, 1965 with the 07.05 City Road to Laisterdyke. *(Brian Myland)*
Bottom: Lostock Hall (Preston)-based Black Five 45226 shunting at City Road in summer, 1967. Another Lostock Hall Black Five, 45347, also worked City Road trips that summer and it appears Low Moor used them on these fill-in turns before they worked back to Lancashire. *(Alan Thompson)*
Right: Like most other main Bradford freight terminals, City Road possessed a large wool warehouse which was equipped with an electric monorail crane for lifting the bales about, as pictured on 6th May, 1959. *(by courtesy of British Rail)*

In February, 1964 City Road staff had to deal with a sticky problem – how to unload liquid detergent which had solidified during its long journey across Europe in freezing temperatures.

The detergent came from Kastl, near Hamburg, Germany, in 20 ton Continental tank wagons for road distribution to local soap and paint firms.

The then area sales supervisor Geoffrey Taylor, goods agent J. Catto and his assistant, Geoffrey Lawson, tackled the problem with a steam heat system.

They got local Outdoor Machinery engineers to rig up a flexible hosepipe from the depot's plant and steam was fed into the tankers which were fitted with internal heating elements.

Top: By 10th June, 1965 when this picture was taken, trains only went as far as Thornton. Here, B1 No.61016 *Inyala* has just passed Horton Junction and is about to go through Horton Park station with the 07.05 pick-up from Laisterdyke which on this day ran only to Great Horton. Towering above are the floodlights of the Park Avenue football ground, home of Bradford FC which lost its Football League status in 1970.

Centre: The same working on 2nd June with 61115 racing its light load through the overgrown Horton Park platforms, closed since 15th September, 1952 but kept intact for occasional football specials.

Bottom: Great Horton station looking towards Bradford on 21st May, 1955 – the last day of passenger services. The goods yard which survived until 28th June, 1965 is to the right. (*Tom Allatt*)

Top: This fine view shows the still busy goods yard at Great Horton, looking towards Bradford, in late 1964. By this time most goods trains were worked by Hammerton Street 204hp diesel shunters like the Class 03 pictured alongside the signal box. (*John Rothera*)

Centre: Three and a half miles from Bradford and a mile south of Queensbury, was Clayton station and its sizeable goods yard, seen looking towards Bradford in 1956. Despite its busy appearance, the goods yard was one of the first on the Queensbury lines to go, closing on 10th April, 1961. (*Peter Sunderland*)

Bottom: Queensbury station and goods yard were already closed and only the goods trains to Thornton remained when BR allowed this Railway Correspondence and Travel Society tour of West Riding branches to venture up the line on 6th September, 1964. Formed of a Calder Valley DMU and a Metro-Cammell unit, it is seen at the Bradford-bound platform of the Keighley line. The Halifax line is on the left. (*Brian Myland*)

Three views of Thornton, on the Keighley line, and how it changed over the space of 10 years.

Top: A J50 0-6-0T shunts the yard while a GNR somersault signal gives the all-clear to a passenger train ready to leave the station for the Queensbury direction on 24th April, 1954. (*H.C. Casserley*)

Centre: Two years later, the station was closed but still intact when seen looking towards Queensbury. (*J.C.W. Halliday*)

Bottom: By the time this picture was taken in spring, 1964, Thornton goods yard was as far as the by now freight only line from Bradford went. Following closure of the next yard along the line at Denholme in 1962, timber traffic for a large joinery firm there was transferred to Thornton and delivered by road, but had all gone by this time. Thornton yard closed on 28th June, 1965 and the track was lifted the following spring. (*John Rothera*)

SHORT MEMORIES

Summer 1966: One of the last Fowler 2-6-4Ts, 42410, is among Huddersfield locos booked for the Bradford–Huddersfield portion of the Bradford/Leeds–Poole train, the loco arriving in Bradford with an early morning newspaper train. Low Moor men not happy with the condition of 42410 often take any other loco available.

September 1966: Work starts on building a new park and ride station at New Pudsey, just west of Stanningley on the intersection between the A647 and A6120 roads.

LOW MOOR

On 15th April, 1961 the Rugby League Cup semi-final between Hull and St Helens was played at the Odsal ground, Bradford, and many special trains were laid on for the supporters of both teams.

Above: No doubt conveying St Helens supporters, train No.1X50 makes for Bradford under the competent charge of Warrington-based unrebuilt Patriot No.45524 *Blackpool*. The engine's excellant condition and patch painting on the boiler suggest it may be ex-works. Below: At least one of the trains from Hull appears to have suffered an engine failure, being headed away from Low Moor towards Bradford by Mirfield 8F 2-8-0 No.48265. Fortunately, the engine was one of those with improved balancing for faster running as indicated by a star beneath the cabside number. (*both Peter Rose*)

This was how Low Moor looked on 15th April, 1961. In 1993 it was an empty wasteland with only the double track Halifax–Bradford line passing through.

The spectacular view was shot from the top of the coaling plant by Peter Rose and shows, from left: the L&Y goods yard, Low Moor No.2 East signal box, the station with a Black Five on a Rugby League special, the ash pits and disposal plant, the 12-road engine shed, turntable and, in the right distance, the railwaymen's cottages which were the only part of this busy centre left intact in 1993. However, Low Moor could rise again. Although plans by BR in 1970 for a Freightliner terminal on the site of the goods yard came to nothing, it has been earmarked since the 1980s for the West Yorkshire Transport Museum which received planning permission in spring, 1993. West Yorkshire PTE also has long term plans for a new station at Low Moor.

Although of L&Y origin, Low Moor shed became notable for the extensive variety of motive power which could be seen there, making it a popular venue for enthusiasts. Not only were there engines from both LMS and LNER camps, but older types from pre-grouping companies like the Great Northern, Great Central, the Midland and the L&Y could be found together as well. In BR days it became home to a sizeable fleet of B1 4-6-0s, two regular performers in the Bradford area in the mid-1960s being 61014 *Oribi* and 61016 *Inyala*, pictured outside the shed by Brian Myland on 15th May, 1965.

Low Moor was coded 25F in the London Midland Region's Wakefield district until being transferred to the North Eastern Region in 1956 when it became 56F, still under Wakefield which became 56A. In summer, 1967 it became 55J for a short time before closing completely on 2nd October, 1967.

LOCOMOTIVES ALLOCATED TO LOW MOOR

Summer, 1950

Fairburn 4MT 2-6-4T: 42107-16/88/9; 5P5F 2-6-0: 42726/7/8/32/828/65; 5MT 4-6-0: 44912/51/90/5201/7/8; L&Y 2P 2-4-2T: 50806; L&Y 3P 2-4-2T:50909; L&Y 2F 0-6-0ST: 51404; L&Y 3F 0-6-0: 52092/104/237/309/410/1/27/61; L&Y 3F 0-6-0: 52590; L&Y 7F 0-8-0: 52857. Total 37.

July 1962

Ivatt 2MT 2-6-2T: 41250/3/63/4/74; Fairburn 4MT 2-6-4T: 42084/107/8/9/16; Fowler 4MT 2-6-4T: 42311/24; Stanier 4MT 2-6-4T:42622; 5MT 4-6-0: 44693/4/5/946/51/90/5207/8; 6P 4-6-0: 45565 *Victoria*/45694 *Bellerophon*; Ivatt 2MT 2-6-0: 46435; 3F 0-6-0T: 47430; B1 4-6-0: 61189 *Sir William Gray* /230/74/383/6/7; J39 0-6-0: 64791/801/72/86/907/19; L1 2-6-4T: 67721/54/9/64; J50 0-6-0T: 68908/22/64/77; WD 2-8-0: 90351/97/711/21/3. Total:50.

November 1966

Fairburn 4MT 2-6-4T: 42055/73/116/84/96; 5MT 4-6-0: 44694/946/51; 6P 4-6-0: 45565 *Victoria*; B1 4-6-0:61115/89 *Sir William Gray*/1309/88; WD 2-8-0: 90711. Total 14.

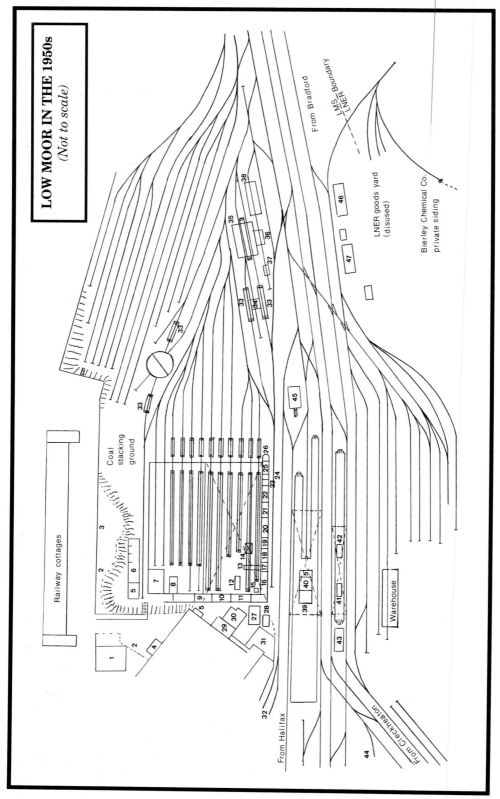

LOW MOOR IN THE 1950s
(Not to scale)

1. Air raid shelter 2. Car park 3. Garages 4. Cycle shed 5. Toilets 6. Dock 7. Canteen 8. New store 9. Boiler smith 10. Tool store 11. Chief mechanical fitter's office 12. Mechanical foreman's office 13. One ton hoist 14. Shearlegs 15. Washing out hydrant 16. Store ground 17. Sand store 18. Sand drying 19. Locker room 20. Fitter's shop 21. Blacksmith's shop 22. Loco stores 23. Drivers' lobby 24. Foreman 25. Clerks 26. Shedmaster 27. Mess 28. Tank 29. Cottage 30. House 31. Compound and store 32. P. Heath and Low Moor Ltd private siding 33. Ash pit 34. Ash lifting plant 35. Mechanical coaling plant 36. Coaling plant tippler 37. Wagon spray 38. Old coaling tank 39. Store room 40. Porters 41. General waiting room 42. Ladies waiting room 43. Low Moor West signal box 44. Carriage sidings 45. Carriage sidings 46. Low Moor No. 2 East signal box 46. Low Moor No. 3 signal box 47. Shunters and inspectors.

Right: On shed on 18th July, 1961 are Fowler 2-6-4T No.42324, Caprotti Black Five No.44754 and, extreme right, L&Y 0-6-0 No.52515. (*Peter Rose*)

Harry Wilson spent 15 years at Low Moor, as a fireman and from the 1950s as a driver. Before that, he was at Wakefield shed but was often loaned to Low Moor, especially for summer Saturday trains to the coast.

"One of our London jobs between 1936 and the start of the war in 1939 was from Bradford Exchange to St Pancras which Low Moor men worked throughout, lodging at Kentish Town before working the corresponding northbound train back the next day.

"We had two Jubilees for this job – *Repulse* and *Warspite* and did the full run in just four hours.

"We left Bradford with only three coaches and picked up a one-coach portion from the Halifax direction at Thornhill. From there we went straight to Sheffield Midland where we took on the Leeds portion which made a train of up to 13 coaches.

"After the war we got the South Yorkshireman, which Low Moor men worked inititially to Leicester, but later only as far as Sheffield.

"We also had jobs to Southport, making 38 stops going out but only four coming back. If we got a Compound it was very hard work with all the stopping and starting.

"There were between 80 and 90 locomen at Low Moor when I was there but towards the end we had very little steam work. Most of the time we were signing on at Bradford to work the DMUs.

"It was very sad when the shed closed though I was lucky to get the only job being transferred to York."

Below: An interesting selection of engines is visible over the end wall of the roofless part of the shed on 15th April, 1961. At the front is WD 2-8-0 No.90200, at least five J39 0-6-0s, Ivatt 2MT 2-6-2T No.41264, and a J50 0-6-0T. (*Peter Rose*)

The large variety of locomotives allocated to Low Moor over the years included, in 1961, some Royal Scots displaced from Leeds Holbeck by diesels.
Above: Keeping company with an ex-LNER Gresley J39 0-6-0 and Black Five No.44695 in the open part of the shed on 18th September was No.46113 *Cameronian*.
Below: On the same day, another Scot was inside the shed. Also rubbing shoulders with a J39 was 46145 *The Duke of Wellington's Regt. (West Riding)*. (both Peter Rose)

More examples of Low Moor variety. **Right:** BR Standard Class 2MT 2-6-2T No.84010 – nearly new and allocated to Low Moor when photographed on shed in May, 1954. These locomotives saw use on Bradford–Penistone trains for a time along with Ivatt Class 2 and Stanier Class 3 2-6-2Ts. (*J.C.Hillmer*)

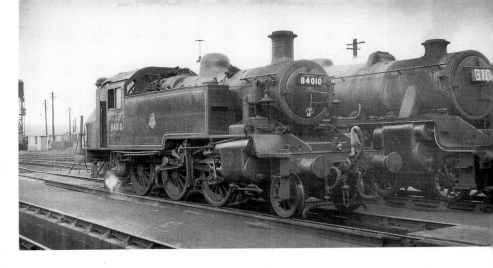

Left: Being one of the principal L&Y passenger depots, Low Moor had a long association with the Aspinall 2-4-2Ts but by May, 1954 when this picture was taken, they had been displaced from front-line work. Standing outside the shed, still with LMS on the tankside, is No.50765 flanked by Crab 2-6-0 No.42704 on the left and another new Standard 2-6-2T, No.84015, (*J.C. Hillmer*)

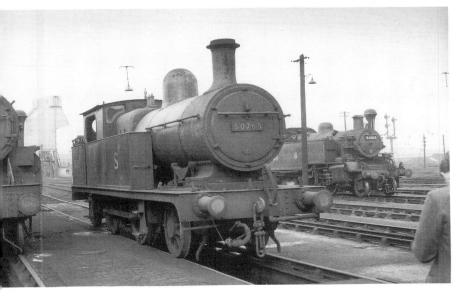

Right: The Wakefield district sheds, Low Moor included, were notable for hosting some of the last surviving Aspinall L&Y 0-6-0s. The class had only a few months left before extinction when Mirfield's No.52121 was found on Low Moor shed on 18th July, 1961. (*Peter Rose*)

Above: Looking towards Bradford from the north end of Low Moor station with Caprotti Black Five No.44746 of Manchester Newton Heath heading for Bradford with a normal service train on 15th April, 1961.

Also in the picture are Patriot 4-6-0 No.45524 *Blackpool*, being coaled after taking its Rugby League special to Bradford, Ivatt 2-6-2T No.41262, stood alongside three old L&Y shunt signals and, in the right distance, a bridge over the closed Great Northern line from Dudley Hill.

Below: Even Deltics made it to Low Moor during autumn, 1961 when Leeds–London trains were diverted because of engineering work. On Sunday, 29th October, No.D9012 *Crepello* heads south through the station, passing Fairburn 2-6-4T No.42116. (*both Peter Rose*)

Top: Another Rugby League special on 15th April, 1961, this time with Hull Dairycoates K3/2 2-6-0 No.61935 passing through platform 2 and overtaking B1 No.61387 in the north-facing bay. (*Peter Rose*)

Centre: The ex-LNER Thompson L1 2-6-4Ts had a spell at Low Moor in the early 1960s after being transferred from Ardsley to replace the J50s. Their braking capacity was not good enough for freight work and 67759 languished unwanted in the snow during February, 1962. In 1949 67761/2 were allocated to Bowling shed and used on Wakefield portions of London expresses until being transferred to Stratford that November. During their stay, 67762 was tested as a new engine on the Queensbury lines. (*Barry Mounsey*)

Bottom: Engineering works on Sunday, 29th October, 1961 saw A4 Pacific 60008 *Dwight D. Eisenhower* rolling a four-coach 12.45pm Leeds to Kings Cross through platform 3 and onto the Cleckheaton line. (*Peter Rose*)

SHORT MEMORIES

5.11.66: Bradford Exchange–Stockport service of two trains each way a day is withdrawn. The morning train is a DMU and the afternoon one a 2-6-4T though the final weeks also see tender engines, Jubilees included. Fairburn 42116 works the service on the last day.

10.6.67: Jubilee No.45697 *Achilles* in poor external condition, hauls the 12.13 Bradford Exchange to Blackpool.

More LNER power at Low Moor.

Above: Waiting at platform 4 with a southbound through freight on 15th April, 1961 was smartly turned out J39 0-6-0 No.64791. Passengers thronged platform 2, indicating that Low Moor was once a busy station before it closed on 14th June, 1965.

Below: The diverted 9.53am Doncaster to Leeds Central comes off the Cleckheaton branch into platform 2 behind B1 4-6-0 No.61016 *Inyala* on Sunday 29th October, 1961. Note the cramped position of the Up Starting signals forced by the close proximity of the junction and signal box. (*both Peter Rose*)

Top: In 1961 there was still a lot of freight on the railway and even on a Saturday like 15th April with special traffic around, it still had to be slotted in. Here, No.64791, one of many ex-LNER engines transferred to Low Moor when Hammerton Street closed to steam, waits in the Up loop with its long through freight. (*Peter Rose*)

Centre: Shunting the goods yard on 11th July, 1957 was yet another variety of engine found at Low Moor – ex-L&Y 2F 0-6-0ST No.51404. Behind it is the long-closed GNR goods shed which, ironically, was the only building apart from the cottages, still standing in 1993. (*Roy Wood*)

Bottom: A DMU running from Bradford to Huddersfield via Heckmondwyke passes Low Moor No.2 West box on Saturday 12th June, 1965. By this time trains did not stop at Low Moor on a Sunday so this was the last day before the station closed. (*Brian Myland*)

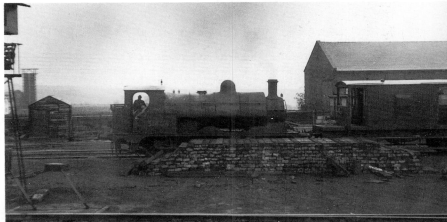

SHORT MEMORIES

9.11.66: Jubilee No.45565 *Victoria* works the 17.15 Bradford Exchange–Rochdale parcels.

27.12.66: Jubilee No.45694 *Bellerophon* works the 09.00 Bradford–Kings Cross relief as far as Wakefield.

23.6.67: B1 No.61306, destined to become the last survivor of its class joins the steam allocation at Low Moor after being transferred from Hull.

23.9.67: 61306 works the 15.17 Bradford Forster Square–Heysham parcels.

Above: Stanier 8F 2-8-0 No.48055 stands on Low Moor South-West curve and awaits the road towards Halifax with a goods off the Cleckheaton branch on 31st March, 1964. The main line to Bradford is on the left while inside the triangle are the carriage sidings, parts of which were still in situ, overgrown and disused for many years, in 1993. (*Michael Leahy*)

Below: Doncaster B1 No.61135 accelarates the diverted 11.20 am Leeds Central to Norwich past Low Moor No.5 box at the Cleckheaton end of the triangle on 29th October, 1961. (*Peter Rose*) Although closing to passengers on 14th June, 1965. the line through Cleckheaton to Thornhill Junction on the L&Y main line near Dewsbury, continued to be used for freight until being severed by motorway construction in 1969. It never reopened due to the decline of freight traffic but there are plans to reopen it as an electric tramway associated with the West Yorkshire Transport Museum.